Horoscope
2021

....

Virgo

24 August – 23 September

igloobooks

igloobooks

Published in 2020
by Igloo Books Ltd
Cottage Farm
Sywell
NN6 0BJ
www.igloobooks.com

0820 001
2 4 6 8 10 9 7 5 3 1
ISBN 978-1-83852-323-7

Written by Belinda Campbell and Denise Evans

Cover design by Simon Parker
Edited by Bobby Newlyn-Jones

Printed and manufactured in China

CONTENTS

. . . .

INTRODUCTION
· · · · · · · · · · · · · · · · · · ·

This 15-month guide has been designed and written to give a concise and accessible insight into both the nature of your star sign and the year ahead. Divided into two main sections, the first section of this guide will give you an overview of your character in order to help you understand how you think, perceive the world and interact with others and – perhaps just as importantly – why. You'll soon see that your zodiac sign is not just affected by a few stars in the sky, but by planets, elements, and a whole host of other factors, too.

The second section of this guide is made up of daily forecasts. Use these to increase your awareness of what might appear on your horizon so that you're better equipped to deal with the days ahead. While this should never be used to dictate your life, it can be useful to see how your energies might be affected or influenced, which in turn can help you prepare for what life might throw your way.

By the end of these 15 months, these two sections should have given you a deeper understanding and awareness of yourself and, in turn, the world around you. There are never any definite certainties, but with an open mind you will find guidance for what might be, and learn to take more control of your own destiny.

THE CHARACTER OF THE VIRGIN

· · · · · · · · · · · · · · · · · ·

As kind as they are critical, as down to earth as they are successful, Virgoans are the perfectionists of the zodiac. They set ideals for everyone, themselves included, to strive towards. Ruled by Mercury, the planet of communication, they will happily offer their opinions on any given subject, both when asked to and when not. Whilst communicating is a forte for many Virgoans, their sharp tongues and analytical brains can mean that their opinions sometimes come across as being overly critical. Extremely detail-orientated, and with the highest of standards, others can seem to fall short by comparison. However, any criticism Virgoans offer will usually be constructive and full of good intentions.

In opposition to neighbouring Leo, the sign of Virgo belongs to the sixth house, which focuses on health and service. Others often look to Virgoans for help and guidance about dieting or big decisions because they know that they will receive practical, informative and candid advice. Virgoans may well be nicknamed 'Dr Phil' (also a Virgoan!) in their group of friends. As well as giving second-to-none counsel, Virgoans are efficient, resourceful and have exceptional attention to detail. Such strong attributes can help Virgoans to become the highest of achievers, but their humility means they are unlikely to let any success go to their heads. Virgoan superstar Beyoncé, for example, is known for her humble attitude despite her incredible accomplishments and global fame. Symbolised by a Virgin, modest and sometimes shy Virgoans will remain as well presented and orderly as their daily to-do lists. They do not usually opt for anything too showy, as is their more introverted, negative way. Born at the end of summer when the leaves begin to transform in colour, Virgoans are a unique combination of certainty, control and change, which allows them to be both organised and organic.

THE VIRGIN

Not to be taken too literally, the symbolic sign of the Virgin represents many qualities in good, yet sometimes naïve, Virgoans. Astraea, the Greek goddess of justice and innocence, makes up the Virgo constellation and is often depicted as the Virgin symbol. However many compliments Virgoans may receive, they will likely remain modest and could come across as shy, giving them an air of innocence that can be highly attractive. This purity can be why they are often seen as being very prim and proper to the outside world, but their qualities are measured best by their ability to always find the good. Virgoans tend to be fair and true thanks to their methodical ability to weigh up the facts with intelligence and honesty, much like Librans. Demeter, the Greek goddess of harvesting, is another deity associated with the Virgin symbol. Holding a sheaf of wheat, Demeter is the mother of Earth's fertility and the reason we have seasons, which is perhaps why mutable Virgoans – with their foresight and love of planning – can make wonderful agriculturists.

MERCURY

The speed at which some analytical Virgoans process information is surely inherited from their ruling planet of Mercury, which orbits the Sun faster than any other planet in the solar system. Mercury is named after the Roman god of the same name, who is typically shown with wings on his head and feet. Virgoans are similarly quick, especially when it comes to thinking. However, the speed at which thoughts race around their heads can mean they sometimes overthink things and obsess over the smallest of details. This can make them hold a grudge better than most. 'Mercury in retrograde' is a phrase that is often met with fearful faces, but what does it mean? Three times a year, Mercury seemingly begins to move backwards and is blamed for many communication, media, technology and travel failures. Whilst many people might avoid making big decisions, signing important documents or arranging trips during a retrograde, ever-practical Virgoans will probably not let their ruling planet slow them down in any significant way.

ELEMENTS, MODES AND POLARITIES

Each sign is made up of a unique combination of three defining groups: elements, modes and polarities. Each of these defining parts can manifest themselves in good and bad ways and none should be seen as a positive or a negative – including the polarities! Just like a jigsaw puzzle, piecing these groups together can help illuminate why each sign has certain characteristics and help us find a balance.

ELEMENTS

Fire: Dynamic and adventurous, signs with fire in them can be extroverted. Others are naturally drawn to them because of the positive light they give off, as well as their high levels of energy and confidence.

Earth: Signs with the earth element are steady and driven with their ambitions. They make for a solid friend, parent or partner due to their grounded influence and nurturing nature.

Air: The invisible element that influences each of the other elements significantly, air signs will provide much-needed perspective to others with their fair thinking, verbal skills and key ideas.

Water: Warm in the shallows and freezing as ice. This mysterious element is essential to the growth of everything around it, through its emotional depth and empathy.

MODES

Cardinal: Pioneers of the calendar, cardinal signs jump-start each season and are the energetic go-getters.

Fixed: Marking the middle of the calendar, fixed signs firmly denote and value steadiness and reliability.

Mutable: As the seasons end, the mutable signs adapt and give themselves over gladly to the promise of change.

POLARITIES

Positive: Typically extroverted, positive signs take physical action and embrace outside stimulus in their life.

Negative: Usually introverted, negative signs value emotional development and experiencing life from the inside out.

VIRGO IN BRIEF

The table below shows the key attributes of Virgoans. Use it for quick reference and to understand more about this fascinating sign.

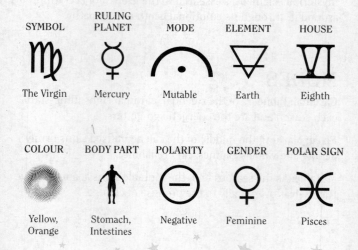

SYMBOL	RULING PLANET	MODE	ELEMENT	HOUSE
The Virgin	Mercury	Mutable	Earth	Eighth

COLOUR	BODY PART	POLARITY	GENDER	POLAR SIGN
Yellow, Orange	Stomach, Intestines	Negative	Feminine	Pisces

ROMANTIC RELATIONSHIPS

· · · · · · · · · · · · · · · · · ·

Virgoans can be choosy lovers. They are not ones to frequently fall in love, but their devotion can last an eternity when finally bestowed on a worthy soul. Anyone chosen by these notoriously picky characters should feel very special indeed. Virgoans can have a tendency to find faults or nitpick about trivial matters, which can be troublesome in love. Wanting to tweak or change minor issues may seem harmless and necessary to mutable Virgoans, but celebrating the differences in their relationships will prove to be far more rewarding than finding flaws. This optimistic outlook of finding the positive needs to extend to themselves too, as they are too often left confused as to what their partners see in them.

Although symbolised by the Virgin, Virgoans are not always naïve when it comes to their relationships. They present themselves impeccably to the outside world with lint rollers at the ready, but they can also be extremely laid-back when they feel at ease in a relationship. When they find themselves in the arms of true love, they will no longer worry about their hair being out of place or their clothes being creased. Curious with a mutable nature, Virgoans are often open to trying new things, which can help keep any long-term flames of love burning brightly. They may struggle initially with exposing themselves to vulnerability, resulting in them not always giving their love freely. However, when Virgoans choose to lower their emotional barriers their endless affection can be well worth the wait.

With a deeply rooted earth element, Virgoans will most appreciate partners who enjoy getting outside and who understand the importance of protecting the planet. Eco-conscious and organised, finding someone who will go trekking in the countryside can be just as important to Virgoans as finding a partner who takes the time to separate the plastic and glass for recycling. Chores aside, they will be the most charmed by someone who brings fun and energy into their meticulously planned lives.

ARIES: COMPATIBILITY 3/5

There's not a lot that's similar about how an Arian and Virgoan think and approach their daily decisions. The Arian rushes in excitedly to almost everything, whereas the Virgoan needs to exhaust all the facts and options first. The Arian can teach the Virgoan the benefits of not getting too bogged down with decisions, and the Virgoan can teach the Arian the equal importance of noticing the smaller details in life. When these two team up, they will understand that they are very, very different, and will likely admire those differences in one another.

TAURUS: COMPATIBILITY 3/5

A Taurean and Virgoan can make for a real power couple. The Taurean's dogged approach to fulfilling goals and the Virgoan's practical and busy mind will see this pair securing a successful future together. The Virgoan can appear overly critical and may end up hurting the Bull's feelings unintentionally. Ruled by Mercury, the planet of communication, the Virgoan can be very attuned to the Taurean's needs and will try to fix any problems within the relationship. These two will likely share many things in common and can form a lifelong companionship, even if a whirlwind romance isn't in the stars.

GEMINI: COMPATIBILITY 1/5

A Virgoan may initially be attracted to a Geminian's charm and wit, but is likely to soon feel irritated by the flights of fancy. The steady Virgoan can feel too reserved for the Geminian, and the fast-paced Geminian can be too unpredictable for the Virgoan. Both ruled by Mercury and strong believers in communication, these otherwise contrasting characters may end up feeling as if they are speaking two completely different languages. However, their mutual love of change and talent for adaptability may well be what makes this relationship last longer than predicted.

CANCER: COMPATIBILITY 3/5

A practical-minded Virgoan could be the balancing force that a Cancerian needs in a partner. The Virgoan will feel loved and protected by the nurturing Cancerian, but by contrast the Cancerian can at times feel hurt by the naturally critical Virgoan. Thanks to ruling planet Mercury, the Virgoan's strong communication skills should help them patch up any problems. The earth element in Virgo and the cardinal influence in Cancer can make for a driven couple, so any loving ambitions that these two share will likely be realised together.

LEO: COMPATIBILITY 2/5

The love of a Leonian can take a Virgoan by surprise; which
isn't something the introverted Virgoan is always keen on. The
clear differences between the studious Virgoan and show-stopping
Leonian can mean that these two might be quick to write each
other off as potential partners at first glance. The relationship
between this fire and earth couple can be a slow burner, but
their slow and steady approach could well end up with these
two winning the race hand in hand. This couple's strengths are
their differences, and these two hard workers can make for a
solid and complementary couple.

LIBRA: COMPATIBILITY 3/5

Both advocates of diplomacy and justice, a Libran and
Virgoan's love should be fair and true. If these two make any
vows together, they will take them very seriously. However,
it is not all contracts and scales in this relationship, as the
Mercury-inspired Virgoan and Venus-ruled Libran could both
have a shared love of beauty and crafts. A date night at a gallery
or the theatre could be perfect for the art-loving Virgoan and
Libran couple. The Libran will have plenty of ideas, and the
practical Virgoan could be the one that helps make those
fancies a reality.

SCORPIO: COMPATIBILITY 5/5

Positioned two places apart on the zodiac calendar, the passionate and loyal bond between a Virgin and Scorpian is a special one. The orderly Virgoan will value the steadiness of the fixed Scorpian, and similarly the loyal Scorpian will appreciate the faithfulness that the Virgoan is known for. With their complementary elements of water and earth and their matching negative energies, this typically introverted couple will enjoy the nourishing effects of spending quality time together. Theirs is an intimate relationship but not without some passionate arguments, thanks to the Scorpian's power-ruled influence of Pluto and the Virgoan's sharp tongue.

SAGITTARIUS: COMPATIBILITY 2/5

These two lovers may really have their work cut out for them. Whilst the outdoorsy Sagittarian and earthy Virgoan both have a strong love for being outside in nature, they have some serious core differences. The Virgoan, for example, loves routine, which the Sagittarian can't abide. Elsewhere, the wild Sagittarian, who gallops heart first towards goals, can sometimes feel too reckless for the overthinking Virgoan, whilst the Sagittarian might find the Virgoan's overactive mind to be a hindrance. If they can find some common ground, this mutable pair could experience an honest and thought-provoking relationship.

CAPRICORN: COMPATIBILITY 4/5

When a hard-working Capricornian and meticulous Virgoan fall in love, there won't be many cracks in their relationship. With the Virgoan's tool kit of practical skills and the Capricornian's portfolio of material achievements, this hard-working couple may well be best at taking on grand projects. Perhaps building their own home somewhere in the countryside would suit this couple, where their shared earth element can be appreciated at its best, and their quieter negative energies embraced. This firm relationship may lack some spontaneity, so thoughtful surprises now and again could help keep the excitement alive.

AQUARIUS: COMPATIBILITY 2/5

An idealist Aquarian and realist Virgoan may not be an obvious match, but this couple can be very happy if they find key ideas and goals to share. The organised Virgoan will appreciate the Saturn-ruled part of the Aquarian that represents structure and order, but less so the rebellious Uranus side that enjoys throwing out the rulebook. The airy Aquarian and Mercury-ruled Virgoan are both freethinkers and should be good at allowing one another room to breathe in the relationship, which both will value. Ultimately, the optimistic Aquarian and the pragmatic Virgoan will need to find a shared ambition to balance out their stark differences.

PISCES: COMPATIBILITY 5/5

Opposites on the zodiac calendar, a hands-on Virgoan and mystical Piscean make a loving match, yet life will not be without the occasional struggle. Water and earth are elements that can create beautiful things together, but in this couple the emotional Piscean and rational Virgoan could be a tricky balancing act. For example, the Piscean sometimes exhibits an elusiveness that can be attractive or frustrating to the steady Virgoan. Overall, however, these two are deep souls that can empathise and support one another probably better than any other match, and can happily and devotedly serve one another for endless days if flexibility and patience is practised by the pair. A fixed and mutable mode can be a complimentary match, so long as Aquarians don't try to bend the will of their accommodating Piscean partner. The bond that these two can share when at its best can be sincere and spiritually liberating.

FAMILY AND FRIENDS

. . . .

It's hard to ruffle unflappable Virgoans, which makes them go-to confidants in times of crisis. Their wise words can be second to none thanks to their honesty and practicality, so offering advice to friends and family is a common practice. Whilst the advice of Virgoans will usually be actively sought, their candid tones can sound callous at times. Even if their intentions are pure, their sharp words can penetrate even the thickest of skins. Virgoans might think that their Cancerian and Scorpian friends have hard shells that can withstand straight talking, for example, but they will actually need to tread lightly because both can be extremely sensitive. After a time, even the most patient of people, such as Taureans, might tire of the Virgoan disapproving tone. To avoid alienating their loved ones, particularly their own children, Virgoans should try to always be constructive rather than overly critical, and give any words of advice without condemnation.

Virgoans' homes most likely reflect their impeccable taste. Their style may be minimal, but it will always be warm. They usually function best if their homes are uncluttered, so if their bedroom is looking disorderly it might be an indication that their thoughts are too. Virgoans can often have a gift for cultivating their earth element, so a house with a garden could be an important feature, whether it's to grow their own organic vegetables or prize-winning roses. Outdoor space or not, Virgoans might decide to bring the outdoors in and decorate every room with plants that will all have been carefully selected to clean polluted air or thrive on sunny windowsills.

Not ones for openly displaying their emotions, Virgoans are more likely to silently sulk until their mood passes. Despite holding stubborn grudges that sometimes feel like a life sentence, Virgoans do forgive and forget with time – as their patient and understanding family and friends will know. Learning to move past bad feeling is essential for Virgoans, as the weight of grievances can start to feel heavy after a while. Opening up to loved ones about how they feel, and letting go of any concerns about vulnerability can be an important first step towards mending any broken bonds and forging stronger friendships. Opposites on the zodiac calendar, Pisceans may well be the emotional key to unlocking the deeper feelings lingering inside of Virgoans.

The social circle of selective Virgoans may be small but strong with lifelong friendships. Whilst they love structure, they suit easy-going and energetic signs that challenge and inspire them. Creative Arians can be the best of friends to crafty Virgoans, and their balance of negative and positive energies are a complementary force that makes for a pioneering and practical alliance.

MONEY AND CAREERS

· · · · · · · · · · · · · · · · · ·

Being a particular star sign will not dictate certain types of career, but it can help identify potential areas for thriving in. Conversely, to succeed in the workplace, it is just as important to understand strengths and weaknesses to achieve career and financial goals.

Thanks to their earth element, some Virgoans may be attached to material objects, but these hard-working types are usually more driven by goals than they are by money. Whilst these overachievers could be destined to make fortunes by reaching the top of their professions, many are known for their thrifty spending habits. Finding sample sales and scouring the Internet for the best insurance deals, frugal Virgoans will only part with their hard-earned money wisely and are unlikely to go on a shopping splurge. Their tendency to over-analyse could leave them struggling with indecisiveness and considering the pros and cons on almost every purchase. This means plenty of time should be allowed when accompanying them on shopping trips.

Wellbeing is of utmost important to Virgoans, so careers based around healthy living could be worthwhile. One profession that they may thrive in could be as nutritionists or cooks like fellow Virgoan chef, Melissa Hemsley. However, if chopping vegetables doesn't appeal, perhaps the health calling that speaks loudest to analytical and cool-headed Virgoans is within medicine, such as becoming doctors or surgeons. Most Virgoans love to work in a neat and pristine environment, so the clinical order of a hospital could be exactly what the career doctor ordered. Whether it's for the operating table or the dinner table, Virgoans will need a clean and chaos-free workstation if they are to function at their very best.

Virgoans can be meticulous and they often excel at finding fault, so any occupation that involves careful checking and solving problems will be a good fit. Working as consultants may well be something that Virgoans come to later in life, once word of their shrewd observation and effective counsel begins to precede them. Virgoans should be wary of their perfectionist ways when striving for improvement, however, as wanting to check and double-check everything can lead to some projects never being completed. Practical-minded Virgoans could benefit from practising a more relaxed viewpoint that finished is sometimes better than perfect.

As with family, colleagues cannot be chosen. Therefore, it can be advantageous to use star signs to learn about their key characteristics and discover the best ways of working together. Born in the sixth house where service can be second nature, Virgoans often excel at both working for, as well as with, other people. Taureans and Capricornians can work doggedly with hard-working Virgoans through the most difficult of tasks, and will bond over their shared grit and determination. Arians, Leonians and Sagittarians are also potentially good workmates, and could help lighten the load with their positive flames by always encouraging their Virgoan colleagues to down tools and take a break.

HEALTH AND WELLBEING

. . . .

A lack of control can make Virgoans feel anxious, but it is essential that they learn to let go periodically so that they don't make life impossible for themselves and everyone around them. Always ready to give others the best of advice, Virgoans should try to listen to their own wise words. However, seeking external professional advice may also be necessary if their need for control is verging on obsessive. Virgoans notoriously love shopping lists, pros and cons lists and to-do-lists, which can quite literally be endless. Writing down worries might free up some mental space for any overactive minds. Learning to take a break may leave Virgoans pleasantly surprised that the world does not collapse when they enjoy a well-deserved day off.

Virgoans can have a reputation for being negative. In some cases this is just them being practical in their unfiltered candid way, however, sometimes it is a fair assessment and should be mended if it is affecting their happiness. An obvious solution to balance out any negative vibe is to counteract it with some feel-good positivity. Virgoans can become stuck on focusing on the negative and lose sight of the positives surrounding them, but if they take the effort to look around they are likely to be able to find something to be grateful for. It could be family or friends, a good hair day, the sun shining outside, the rain watering the garden, and so on. Spending time with optimistic Sagittarian friends or family members could also be the positive injection that Virgoans need to boost them on a down day.

Virgoans can be incredibly health conscious, and often take extra care of their mental, physical and spiritual health.

However, sometimes this can verge on hypochondria. Maybe it's because Virgoans are good at noticing the little things that makes them so alert to their bodily health, but their Internet history is probably littered with online searches desperately trying to self-diagnose the latest potential rash. Scaring themselves with Internet diagnoses is probably a common occurrence, so registering with a local doctor should be the number one priority whenever Virgoans move home. They may well be on a first-name basis before long, but they are always happy to add another name to their Christmas card list. Virgoans generally take such good care of themselves that they should hopefully not have too many reasons to visit the doctor's. Associated with the stomach, Virgoans may wish to take extra care of this area by eating a gut-friendly diet, and easing any anxieties that might be tying their insides into knots.

Virgo

....

DAILY FORECASTS
for 2020

OCTOBER

. . . .

Thursday 1st

October begins with a Full Moon. This will illuminate areas in your life where you have been trying to create endings and new beginnings. Subjects you find uncomfortable to think about are at the forefront now, but you know that there is a need to make a decision. What will you do?

Friday 2nd

Venus enters Virgo, helping to bring beauty and harmony to your outward appearance. You may change your hair colour or buy a new outfit. Elsewhere, you may attract more people into your life, and be able to persuade and coerce them to get what you want. Be sure you don't take advantage of anyone's goodwill, however.

Saturday 3rd

You can afford a little luxury right now, so why not indulge yourself? Spend on good food or something new for your home. There is a fantastic energy that you should make the most of. Feeling good, looking good and fulfilling your needs are the themes of the day, and will put you in an excellent mood for the days ahead.

Sunday 4th

You should be prepared for some emotional baggage to find its way to the surface today. There may be some conversations about past issues that rise up and shock your foundations. You could be left feeling unstable. Deal with what comes up and do not push it back down.

Monday 5th

A positive energy will return, as all three planets in your creative sector are now direct. This bodes well for falling in love, self-expression and art projects. Children will also feature, and laughter, play and joy return to this area for you. You can aim high and succeed now, so enjoy yourself.

Tuesday 6th

Put your energy into work today. Working on a project with a partner could be satisfying, and you may see solutions where others cannot. Your ability to look at things from all angles will benefit your career and make for a productive day. Check all the small details, sometimes apparently insignificant things can make all the difference in the long run.

Wednesday 7th

Mercury and Uranus are facing each other in your communications and travel sectors, which means you may be able to easily discuss unusual subjects or to surprise people. This connection could also mean that somebody will speak unwanted words and cause upsets and disagreements. Don't be that person. Keep your head down and keep the peace.

Thursday 8th

Phone a friend or ask the audience. Advice from your social network will be soothing, so seek it out. Home comforts and motherly love can be acquired from friendship circles. Spend time with close friends who understand your needs and make you feel at home. Those who know you best will welcome your presence.

Friday 9th

There could be a confrontation owing to the warrior and power energy being generated by Mars and Pluto. With Mars sitting in your sex sector and Pluto in your love sector, this dispute could take place in one of your key relationships. Venus, in your area of self, can lend the love to soothe the situation and smooth down any ruffled feathers. Try not to hold onto anything negative which comes out of today.

Saturday 10th

You may not be able to find the energy for creative pursuits today. Instead, you may just want to spend time with friends or on social media. Watch out for someone trying to rock the boat and cause unrest. This could hurt deeply, so it is best avoided. Lie low.

Sunday 11th

There is a restless urge to do something but also do nothing. You cannot settle on a task or think clearly. Hide yourself away and enjoy a film and some ice cream. Taking the time to relax and be alone will help guide you through this anxious energy. Sometimes resting can feel like a waste of time, but you can't look after others if you don't look after yourself first.

Monday 12th

Today is best spent focusing on where you are, at this moment, instead of times gone by. Your mind could be pulled into thoughts of the past and unfinished business. Practise mindfulness and observe where your thoughts are leading without acting on any of them. There is no point dwelling on the past. Instead, acknowledge it and move forwards.

Tuesday 13th

The Moon comes into Virgo, which will help you to review how you serve your community. What do you do out of love? What do you do out of duty? You can be a guiding light for others when you are on top form, so make sure you take time to look after yourself and don't take on too much. Others appreciate your wisdom.

Wednesday 14th

Mercury begins another retrograde period, and he does so in your communication sector. Review recent conversations or investigations into subjects that you became interested in. Are they working out for you? Transform recent findings into something more useful. Make return visits to newly discovered places, what other treasures can you find there?

Thursday 15th

You must look at your finances today. Is there something that you can buy, sell or even invest in? There could be a recent investment that no longer looks like a good deal. Note it, but don't do anything about it until after Mercury retrograde. Rash decisions are not always helpful for maintaining stability, and could make things worse instead of better.

Friday 16th

You have a New Moon in your finance sector. This sector also deals with your home and possessions. If there is a home improvement project you've been thinking about, now is the time to put plans into action. You may also be considering sharing your home with another person.

Saturday 17th

This could be a day filled with words. The Moon is making connections to Mercury and Uranus, which suggests that sentiments expressed verbally may come out unfiltered. You may say something that you later regret. Try to use this energy for written communication instead, which will give you time to assess your thoughts before you send them. Read and research interesting subjects.

Sunday 18th

A lesson is waiting for you, so be prepared to listen to it carefully and take it on board. Some light is shed on your creative sector that requires attention. You can manage this with great compassion if you are considerate, and this will benefit all involved. This lesson is sent by Saturn, so you had best learn it thoroughly.

Monday 19th

A matter of the heart or project that you are passionate about will get a dual hit from Venus and Mars. Venus will put her heart and soul into it as a passion project, but Mars wants to destroy it and forget about it, giving you the opportunity to start fresh with a clean slate and new endeavour. Whichever way you act, it will be on a Jupiter-sized scale.

Tuesday 20th

Stop digging up the past. You may be like a dog with a bone right now and will not let something go. It could be playing on your mind and tugging at your heart. Leave it alone, there's no value in raking up old issues and causing unrest over things you can do nothing about. This will ultimately cause chaos, so put it down and step away.

Wednesday 21st

You will be able to get some measure of control back today. You have found what you want, filed it away and are now researching what you are going to do about it. Yesterday's extreme emotions have calmed down and you are feeling in a better place for making decisions about the future. There is gold in what you've found. Hold on to it safely.

Thursday 22nd

There's still a lot of tension in the air, but you'll have to get used to it as it's not leaving just yet. The Sun has entered your communications sector and is heating up the already-hot topics you love so much. Try not to get carried away, as others may not share your enthusiasm in this matter. You might have to bring something to a close.

Friday 23rd

Health checks are needed now. You may be emotionally drained and this will affect your physical wellbeing. Mercury retrograde is making himself heard and may have already upset your daily routines. Slow down or step back. You need to look after yourself first and foremost. Rest is never wasted time if it helps you to get back to your best self.

Saturday 24th

Venus is in your area of self today and is pleading with Saturn to go easy on you. You are sometimes too hard on yourself and can feel guilty about wasting time, but you shouldn't worry. You don't have to do everything yourself, or keep stretching yourself thin across too many commitments. Instead, review and assess your personal boundaries. You cannot be there for everyone.

. . . .

Sunday 25th

Mercury is in the full heat of the Sun today, in your communications sector. You may want to let off some steam. Be warned, Mercury is still retrograde and you're likely to cause or get involved in arguments because of it. Reign it in, try not to overstep, and maybe you will get through this without rocking the boat too much. Watch out for someone trying to fool you.

Monday 26th

The Moon is in your relationship sector and is making great connections for a lovely time with a special person. You can relate well with surprising ease. This can be a pleasant time and a little respite from Mercury's antics. Go and do something sweet with a loved one, enjoy some quality time without the stress of the retrograde.

Tuesday 27th

Today, you can drift off nicely into fantasy lands with a partner or close friend. Talking about shared dreams and visions could be a fun activity, and open up new possibilities for the future. Lovers will want to merge and singletons will desire a spiritual connection. Meditation or prayer will nourish your soul.

Wednesday 28th

Venus enters your money sector today, alongside retrograde Mercury. You now have two personal planets bookending this sector. Venus is in her home sign, so she will bring her gifts of money, harmony and self-worth. Mercury wants to take a deeper dive and review these issues. Allow them both to guide you through this.

Thursday 29th

The Moon meets Mars in your sex, death and rebirth sector today. He is still slowly retrograding here, and this is why you haven't felt any progress in this area. End something now. This is a reminder from the Moon that it will be an emotional loss, but it is for the best.

Friday 30th

Travel and adventure are now on your mind. You're eager to move on and explore somewhere new, but concrete plans keep crumbling. Maybe this is just not meant for you right now. Take a look at something closer to home like higher education. Perhaps you could learn a new language.

Saturday 31st

Today is a Blue Moon day, which means it is a second Full Moon in one calendar month. This occurs in your travel sector and right on top of Uranus, the disruptor. Make a wish and see what needs to change. This is the right time to let something go, and free up space for new and exciting endeavours.

NOVEMBER

· · · · · · · · · · · · · · · · · · ·

Sunday 1st

You are still reeling from yesterday's Full Moon. However, the Moon has moved on and is making a great connection to Jupiter in your creative sector. You will feel emotionally attached towards to large new projects and will be feeling very positive about them. Lucky Jupiter is on your side.

Monday 2nd

You may be thinking about your career. Contemplate how far you've come, or have you not made the progress you wanted? Is this your vocation at all? Is this right for you? The voice of conscience is likely to tell you to concentrate and get on with it. Consider your options and plans for the future, set yourself goals to make them happen.

Tuesday 3rd

This could be a very harmonious day, as the Moon is holding both Venus and Mars in a friendly embrace. Encounters with the opposite sex will go smoothly, especially workplace connections between male and female colleagues. Equality is the theme of the day.

Wednesday 4th

Mercury finishes his retrograde today and will go back over the last section of your money area. This may leave you pondering financial commitments or contracts that need to be signed. Anything you may have reviewed in this area will now come back up to be dealt with, once and for all.

Thursday 5th

Now is the time when you want to see your friends and feel like part of a tribe which knows you well. You may want to put money into joint investments or spend on a big night out with your social groups. This isn't a good idea. Resist the urge to spend too much. Instead, try to connect without the fuss, perhaps over a dinner at home, or a cosy movie night.

Friday 6th

Plans for a group holiday or expedition may begin to take shape today. However, they will not go smoothly as this travel will eventually be disrupted in some way. Social network groups could become aggressive and you may see some online fighting. Do your very best to remain neutral, you don't need to be dealing with drama on the internet.

Saturday 7th

Take this weekend for yourself. The Moon in your dreaming sector brings restlessness or laziness. Either way, you will not be very good company. You may be pacing the floor wondering what to do and become a bear with a sore head when you can't decide. Meditation or mindfulness may help you focus, and some exercise could help combat the restlessness and let you unwind properly.

Sunday 8th

The energy today is stuck and unmoving. As it's a Sunday, this doesn't matter too much. You may become irritable and attempt to do different chores, but nothing will actually be completed. Getting stuck into a good book is the best thing you can do. Allow yourself the time to be still, you deserve a break too!

Monday 9th

There will be disharmony between men and women today.
This could also be about money that is yours versus money
or financial commitments that you share with another. Take
stock of things and ensure you know where the boundaries are.
Power struggles and control issues will unsettle you.

Tuesday 10th

The Moon is in your sign of self, meaning every little slight
will be felt sharply and be taken personally. Try to let things
go instead of storing up hurts which were not meant that way.
There's tension in the air that you cannot deal with. Mercury is
in the last degree of your money sector and is urging you to tie
up any unfinished business.

Wednesday 11th

Today is buoyant and lively, which is a relief after yesterday's
tense atmosphere. Expressing your needs and being your
unique self comes easily. Enjoy the opportunity to get on with
any creative projects or things that you are passionate about
now. If you show people what you are made of, you cannot fail.

Thursday 12th

The Moon and Venus are sitting together in your money and
home sector. You will delight in this environment and enjoy
being in your own space. Money may come in or be spent well.
Big changes are going on in your creative sector and these will
bring big benefits. It's a good day for you, so enjoy the energy
and be pleased with yourself.

Friday 13th

Today, you are likely to have the type of conversations that most people are afraid of. Tread carefully and be sure not to push further than others are comfortable with. Research and education can be about esoteric subjects. How might you transform a passion into something that will bring you greater status? This is your time to shine.

Saturday 14th

Mars finally goes direct in your sex, death and rebirth sector. Now is the time to make those big changes and clear the decks for something new to come in. You may be backtracking on a decision made earlier this year that has not gone as expected, but this is a positive change. Get ready for new opportunities.

Sunday 15th

The New Moon in your communications sector will allow you to investigate deeper topics. There is an urge to learn something new, but this could be something related to your past rather than anything which your future might hold. Now is the time to dig for gold in your psyche and bring it to the forefront to work on.

Monday 16th

Be careful with financing your new interests today, as your passion and enthusiasm may translate into overspending. Venus is trying to rein you in before it gets out of hand. Jupiter is involved here too, which means that any debts could become unmanageable. Pace yourself, and remember that not everything has to be bought right now. Save up instead, and spend prudently.

Tuesday 17th

This is one of those days where you must put your money where your mouth is or remain silent. Shock revelations, secrets or talking about taboo subjects will not reflect well on you, so it's better to keep quiet. Discretion is the better part of valour, after all. More positively, this influence may make you a more inventive and original thinker.

Wednesday 18th

Mars is eager to pick up speed in your sex, death and rebirth sector but is being held back. This is because his forwards motion is often coupled with aggression and force. March onwards with love and be mindful of others, gentleness will never go amiss in these matters. Is there something you need to complete?

Thursday 19th

There's a lesson to be learnt today in your communications sector. You may be attending a class or lecture to learn about a topic that is regarded by others as unusual, but don't let outside judgement make you cautious. Throw your heart into your creative work and watch the fascinating results. This is a very interesting day for you.

Friday 20th

Right now, daily routines need attention. This may annoy you, as they no longer have the same appeal as new things in your life. This will make you feel burdened and chained. You may well throw a tantrum in an attempt to get your own way, but it won't work. We all have to do the boring work sometimes, so the sooner you get it done, the sooner you can enjoy your new passions.

Saturday 21st

Two planets shift signs, and with them come plenty of positive feelings. The Sun is moving into your family sector, bringing back the warmth and laughter of your loved ones. Venus is entering your communications sector, lending harmony and beauty to conversations and intellectual interests. You will find the gold that you went searching for recently.

Sunday 22nd

This is a wonderful day for being with a special person. The Moon is entering your relationship area, allowing you to switch off and enjoy couple time, so make the most of it if you can. This could also be a great opportunity to connect with your spirit, so practise yoga, meditation or just have a peaceful time pursuing activities you love. Enjoy this energy.

Monday 23rd

The Moon is sitting right on top of Neptune, and it may feel as though you have been washed away to a tropical island. This energy could also mean that you will become lost in the deep blue sea of daydreams and fantasies. Keep one foot on solid ground. Fantasy and illusion can be intoxicating, but you have responsibilities in the real world which can be far more rewarding for you.

Tuesday 24th

Mercury may save you from drowning in thoughts today with his incessant questions. You want to know the whys and wherefores of life and death. Slow down and swim to the shore. The answers will not be found in a sea of words. Ground and centre yourself first.

Wednesday 25th

You're eager to get on with exploring the greater mysteries of life. Recent dreaminess now has more common sense, and you will be able to follow paths on solid ground. You will become increasingly motivated, and full of ideas and places you would like to conquer. Now that these dreams are built on the foundations of reality, they have a chance of succeeding.

Thursday 26th

Your drive and energy will get a boost from hot-headed Mars, and you may feel more focused than you did before. However, be careful not to accompany this with Mars' tendency to be aggressive, as that could hurt rather than help you in your goals. You have the willpower to start projects but may lose interest in them quickly.

Friday 27th

Venus, the planet of love and money, is opposite Uranus, the planet of disruption, today. These are both in sectors to do with money and travel. Be warned that this could mean arguments or unrest around these themes, perhaps holiday plans or shared investments. A compromise is needed, what allowances can you make to ensure peace? If you cannot come to an agreement, find a way to transmute the tension.

Saturday 28th

A grounded Moon in your travel sector may make you somewhat unmoving and stubborn today. Try not to be too immovable, though. The Moon is connecting to Neptune in your relationship sector, who may want to deceive you. Don't let the wool be pulled over your eyes. Stay alert for anything or anyone that does not feel real.

Sunday 29th

There will be a lot of conversation today, and you may lose your voice. This energy also means that someone else may be doing all the talking and getting on your nerves. Someone could even be boasting or exaggerating. Egos could become inflated now, so keep yours under control.

Monday 30th

Today is a Full Moon and partial lunar eclipse in your career sector. There may be unorthodox dealings going on under the eclipse shadow. Is there someone who is not playing fair at work? You may learn something today about boundaries and where they have been crossed.

DECEMBER

· · · · · · · · · · · · · · · · ·

Tuesday 1st

Mercury is entering your family sector. As the build-up to the festive season is here, Mercury can be an ally in making plans with family. This time of year can also bring tension with loved ones, so use Mercury's energy well and make sure that everyone is on the same page before everything starts.

Wednesday 2nd

There may be some early celebrations with friends today. You feel more comfortable with them than with family. They nurture you, or perhaps it's you who is nurturing them? You may feel irritable or vulnerable at this time. A friendly embrace from someone who understands you is sure to put it right. Be thankful for your tribe of friends.

Thursday 3rd

You may feel moody and vent your irritability on, or with, friends. Part of you wants to leave a situation or get a new one started but you don't have the support to do so. This is just a passing Moon phase, so do not act on it. Instead, work out what is a long term issue to address in future, and what is just the symptom of a bad mood.

Friday 4th

Time alone is the best medicine now. You may feel like a caged animal pacing up and down. When the Moon is in your dream sector, as it is today, you often feel restless. Are you doubting yourself? Take the day or evening to relax. Exercise or meditation should help you to settle.

Saturday 5th

Your restlessness will mutate into immobility today. Emotionally, you want to erupt like a volcano but are keeping it all bubbling under the surface. Let it go or do something productive with it, such as painting or baking. Alternatively, use today to spritz the house ready for the festive season. Don't let it fester and spread.

Sunday 6th

There will be a lovely connection between Venus and Neptune today, which is great for romance and connecting with a partner. Heads and hearts can be aligned now. Relationships are harmonious and time spent together can be cosy and enjoyable. The Moon will move into Virgo this evening, adding to the warm atmosphere.

Monday 7th

Be prepared for a nice surprise. This could be an early Christmas gift, or perhaps an unexpected visitor. There is also the potential to surprise yourself. You may feel or do something that is unusual for you, but it might help you see new opportunities. This is a hidden side, but it needs to be shown because it's really very nice.

Tuesday 8th

You may have more passion for creative projects now, so make the most of this energy to work on something you love. If there's anything you want to say, it will be well received. This is a super energy, and you need to roll with it and allow it to expand your chest with pride. Remember to give yourself a clap for something well done.

Wednesday 9th

You may need to organise things around the home today, and your house may benefit from a bit of feng shui. There will be communication with family members but be wary of being dragged into something that you don't want to do. Stand by your boundaries and don't allow others to make demands on your time if you cannot feasibly afford it. What looks like a good idea might not be, so tread carefully.

Thursday 10th

The fog is shifting from a difficult situation today. This is not a big issue, but it may involve some manipulation so tread carefully and watch out for deceptions. Beware of seductive talk that could lead you astray. Venus, who is in your communications sector, is embracing Pluto in your love and creative sector. You should be able to express yourself to a romantic partner or through your art.

Friday 11th

You will get an energetic boost today, helping you to march into muddier ground. You want to get to the bottom of an issue, excavate it and see what it is all about. Do you really want to be dragging up the past now? Is this a good idea? Think before you act. Sometimes there is no value in dredging up old issues, and if there is no chance of progress is there any point in rehashing old ground?

Saturday 12th

The Moon is meeting Venus in your communications sector today, where they can talk about the mysteries of life and death. They are likely to tell each other secrets but these may not be theirs to share. Beware of gossipers, and do not be the one spilling the beans about another.

Sunday 13th

A family gathering could be fun, and you will enjoy the company of outgoing people with an enthusiasm for travel, so try to gather your nearest and dearest around you. People interested in higher education will also interest you, and they could have valuable knowledge to share. This could be a time for telling stories around the campfire. Have fun and let everyone take a turn.

Monday 14th

Today brings a fiery New Moon in your family sector. This Moon also sits with Mercury on a point that is about the past. You can expect a lot of reminiscing about your ancestors' paths. Who are the pioneers in your family? How can you likewise move on? What lessons can you learn from them?

Tuesday 15th

Venus is gliding into your family sector after making an exciting connection with Jupiter. This will infuse love, beauty and harmony into your family relations right on time for the festive celebrations. You may feel enthusiastic and lively now, and ready to party. Travel plans are on your mind, and you may research new places to visit.

Wednesday 16th

Today, your heart may tell you that there's something out there for you that is pure gold. However, it will come with a price. Are you willing to pay it? Is it worth the price tag? Make sure you are ready for this. You may chase dreams and manifest them into realities, but there is something you need to let go or transform first. Don't let this opportunity slip by.

Thursday 17th

There's a sense of Alice in Wonderland in the air today. The Moon is visiting Jupiter, which will leave you feeling swollen with joy, perfect for a season of gifts and goodwill. Later, the Moon will also meet the great teacher Saturn, and you will feel small again. This could feel very surreal. Embrace it, do not fear it. It's good to remember you're part of something bigger.

Friday 18th

Saturn is moving into your health and duties sector today and will stay here for the next two-and-a-half years. There will be huge lessons to learn now. Saturn is about boundaries, so you will need to consider where your limits are in what you do for others. Prime health is important now, so make sure you take care of yourself as well as others.

Saturday 19th

Jupiter is at the final degree of your love and creativity sector, lending a sense of urgency and anticipation to the air. Finalise something big and important in this area. You may feel romantic and could make a grand, last-minute gesture. Is everything ready for Christmas? Maybe you could use this energy to get things in place.

Sunday 20th

There's a frantic energy today that could feel like a push-and-pull exercise regime. This is the result of Jupiter and Saturn sitting together in your health and duties area. The best thing you can do is go to the gym or do some fitness training. Push, pull and breathe. You'll feel better and it might clear your head, putting you in the right frame of mind for the coming days.

Monday 21st

The longest and darkest night is here. The Winter Solstice marks the Sun and Mercury moving into your love and creativity sector. This can herald cosy nights with a lot of talking. How do you like the thought of being locked away for winter to make beautiful art or poetry?

Tuesday 22nd

You may get a little too close for comfort with someone today. You or another will be digging for secrets or wanting to take a relationship further. This could be as simple as planning a holiday together, but you may not be ready for that. Intimacy could be unwanted now.

Wednesday 23rd

The tension is rising just before the celebrations. There may be issues of aggression and control, which you will feel deeply. People around you will fight for the right to be in charge of the festivities. Let them carry on, it isn't your fight and you don't need the stress. Stick to your guns and do not get involved. Focus on your own projects and try to ease your way through to Christmas.

Thursday 24th

Yesterday's tensions may now make you want to run away and hide until the air clears, but this isn't possible. This makes you feel very uncomfortable, but unfortunately you simply have to see it out. You may feel resentful over the hold someone has over you. Do some grounding exercises and hold on tight. This could be a bumpy ride.

Friday 25th

Merry Christmas! You might have to put on a festive front today even if you don't quite feel it. Volatile emotions will still be bumping around as the Moon settles on disruptive Uranus. Speech may be unfiltered and come out with no regard for the consequences. You will feel duty-bound to see the celebrations out before making your escape. Don't get involved in any arguments, and try not to take things personally.

Saturday 26th

Today is much quieter as people have withdrawn to lick their wounds. You're thankful for the respite, so take some time to relax in your own space. Fathers and sons are implicated in the recent tension but mothers step in now as peacemakers. There may well be an illusion of peace thrown over the whole day.

Sunday 27th

If you have brought any work home for the break, now is the time to do it. You need to retreat and take your mind off of Christmas, and feel like you are still in touch with normal life. Getting absorbed in filing, statistics, analysis, or even general work or life administration ready for the new year will make you feel like you again, if only for a few hours.

Monday 28th

You will need to keep family at arm's length today. Venus is doing her best to bring back harmony, but an opposing Moon is making everyone moody still. Bridges are being built and bumpy roads are being smoothed over but this is not an easy task. If you were responsible, own it and repair it. Perhaps being bottled up together is exacerbating these moods. If possible, see if you can get out in the fresh air and let it blow away the angst.

Tuesday 29th

A Full Moon in the sign that rules mothers means that you will need to take care of those who have been hurt in the recent tensions. If you are the injured party, take refuge with friends or online groups who will listen without judgement and provide support. This Moon will illuminate the problems that need healing now.

Wednesday 30th

Your thoughts and feelings are not in synch today, so it's best to keep them to yourself. There are still some illusions, or possibly even outright lies around you. You feel like switching off and retreating. This is absolutely fine. Take it easy. Things are heading back towards normal routine again, and should hopefully settle down soon.

Thursday 31st

New Year's Eve could be an anti-climax this year, but that might be a relief. Issues could get out of hand, so you must stay alert tonight. Struggles with men may happen, while women may seem to want to live in the past. Be the better person and go into 2021 with an abundance of compassion for everyone. If you want to celebrate the new year quietly and without drama, do so. Don't be pressured into bigger plans if you're not in the mood.

Virgo

DAILY FORECASTS
for 2021

JANUARY

Friday 1st

Happy New Year and welcome to 2021! The Moon is in your hidden sector. You may feel deflated or resentful that you didn't get to enjoy the evening as you would have liked. Your ruler Mercury has a dreamy conversation with Neptune. This sounds like love talk.

Saturday 2nd

Take some time to brood or simply be alone today. There is a rush for action in your intimacy sector but you're not feeling up to it. Mars asks that you ensure that your goals for the year are set in stone this week. Sit with your planner and do admin or make checklists.

Sunday 3rd

The Moon comes into your sign and your mind is busy filtering information. You may already be in back-to-work mode. If you have party food left over, enjoy it with friends or someone special. You can reward yourself with a treat after doing your paperwork today.

Monday 4th

You are keen to declutter or cleanse things around you. It's likely that you aren't seeing the full picture concerning your personal relationships right now as Neptune sits in this sector with a mist around him. Perhaps this is the clutter you wish to get rid of. You need clarity.

Tuesday 5th

The Moon shifts into your finance and values sector. January can always feel grey and stretched after the Christmas spending. Aim to balance your bank accounts and ensure you have what you need in your home today. You don't want to be running out to the late-night shop. Mercury meets Pluto and they discuss a transformation project you must do.

Wednesday 6th

Mars is in his final day of your intimacy sector. There is a sense of urgency now. Did you manage to get to the bottom of that mystery? Did you exert too much pressure getting to know someone more deeply? You have a last chance to put this right today, but don't overstep others' boundaries for the sake of your own closure. Be considerate.

Thursday 7th

Mars now moves onto your travel sector, tempting you with exciting trips to get away from January's cold, dark nights. While he's here you will have a keen interest in tasting the exotic delights of a foreign culture. You may plan a trip, a course of higher education or simply get to know people from a different culture. This will excite you.

Friday 8th

The Moon moves into your communications sector. You can be quite the detective and search every corner for the information you need. It's likely that you come across as nosey or gossipy now so be careful not to tread on any toes. Do research for the right reasons.

. . . .

Saturday 9th

Your ruler, Mercury flies into your health and duties sector.
Your tasks and daily chores will increase and you'll fly through
your days with ease. Venus moves into your creative sector;
expect words of love and a boost to your self-worth while she
is here.

Sunday 10th

Time spent with family today can be interesting, if you are
open to the lessons being taught. You may be asked to take on
a new responsibility which will at first repel you. This will feel
like a restriction on your personal time and energy but may,
in fact, turn out to be beneficial. Give it some thought before
committing. Look at the pros and cons objectively, rather than
instinctively turning it down.

Monday 11th

Having just met Saturn, Mercury now meets Jupiter. You begin
to feel more optimistic about this new obligation you have
been presented with. Whereas Saturn made you think small,
Jupiter shows you how this will open your opportunities.
Where Jupiter is involved, things get bigger, talk this through
with as many people as you can.

Tuesday 12th

Mercury is squaring off with Uranus today. Uranus likes to
disrupt the status quo so expect a shake-up or a tantrum. Be
careful not to let your tongue loose against those who don't
deserve it. Alternatively, you may come up with a bold, new
idea and solve a problem.

Wednesday 13th

A New Moon occurs today in your creative sector. If there's
something you are passionate about, set goals today to make
time for it. This may be a slow-growing project or love affair.
You may not feel you have the energy for it today, but this will
change. Making time for things you love is just as important as
your commitments to others.

Thursday 14th

The planetary energy is conflicting. The Sun and Pluto meet
in your creative sector. This can feel like a power struggle or a
beautiful transformation. The Moon in your health and duties
sector meets Mercury and Jupiter, making you emotionally
drained but sure of how to move forward. You may be tired,
but this is a positive step.

Friday 15th

A lovely, connection-free Moon helps you to think about how
you are serving the greater good, although you may waver
between resentment and heroism. Doing something willingly
for a very good reason is an honour, but doing something
which is making you resentful can backfire in the long term.
You, of all signs, can see this eventually. Schedule it into
your planner.

Saturday 16th

The Moon is in your opposite sign and this is time for merging
with your partner or other important relationships. You're
much more inclined to be dreamy and unrealistic now. Your
ideals and that of another need to meet somewhere in the
middle for you to align yourself with this partnership. Make
sure you express yourself clearly.

Sunday 17th

The Moon meets Neptune today. This energy makes you consider surrendering to the natural flow of relationships. Sacrifice and surrender are not the same. Don't compromise yourself in your quest for peace, particularly if those around you aren't also making an effort. Your day may be interrupted by your duties and you are resentful about this. Listen to those who know best.

Monday 18th

The week begins with you having a head full of ideas. There is far more to life than you can ever grasp, but you wish to begin somewhere, so here is as good a place as any. Your eye for detail spots flaws in theories about life, death and rebirth and you wish to examine them more. Spend your day getting philosophical, but don't let it distract you too much from the here and now.

Tuesday 19th

Romantic endeavours don't go so well today as your heart is seeking comfort elsewhere. Your ruler is keeping your mind busy with revolutionary ways of getting through your daily routines with ease. Make notes and assess these at a later date as they may come in handy.

Wednesday 20th

Two volatile planets meet up today. Mars and Uranus are getting hot and bothered in your travel sector. It's possible that you've given yourself too many projects this year and are already feeling the pinch. The Sun moves into your health and duties sector, wait and see if a solution is illuminated.

Thursday 21st

The Moon now meets up with Mars and Uranus. This feels emotionally draining and you're close to having a tantrum or a showdown with someone. Saturn is standing back and watching what you do. Be an adult about this, don't let your inner child rule. Arguments can only cause hurts, rather than solving problems in the long run.

Friday 22nd

Today is an easier day than others lately, as Venus helps to soothe you. You must realise that you are valued and loved. Don't listen to your inner critic as this is Mercury playing his tricks with you. You are valuable, you are loved, and you are doing your best. If you need to bring something to an end to lighten your load, do it. Making time for self-care is important.

Saturday 23rd

You have much to think about at the moment. The Moon moves into a chatty area of your chart and you find yourself networking and asking for advice with your elders or bosses. Listen to what they have to say, as they can guide you towards your end goals. Venus and Neptune combine to let you have a chance of romance and relaxation.

Sunday 24th

For the first time this year, the Moon crosses the point of fate. This monthly visit is when you take time to consider where your future lies, so you could start to make a plan for the year ahead. The Sun meets Saturn in your health and duties sector and reminds you to check in with your body and attend to any health problems you may have.

Monday 25th

Mars and Jupiter are squaring off. Whatever mood you find
yourself in today will be greatly exaggerated by Jupiter's
influence. By evening, the security of your own home beckons.
The Moon is now in your social sector and you need your
friends to nurture you.

Tuesday 26th

You can be defensive and snappy with your social groups.
Take note of what triggers you and try to understand why. Do
you always need to be right? Let this go and allow your wider
friendship groups to make you feel at home and protected.
Acknowledging you can be wrong can give you valuable
opportunities to grown and learn. Don't bite the hand that
feeds you.

Wednesday 27th

The Moon sits opposite Venus and Pluto today. This influence
can make you suspicious about the people you call friends.
Neptune is dragging you away to spend time with a lover or
business partner. This may be just the thing you need to come
back into balance with yourself. Remember to breathe and
don't act rashly. Actions taken in haste are repented at leisure.

Thursday 28th

A Full Moon in your hidden sector makes things tricky today.
You will see control issues coming from all angles. This lunar
month will highlight where you aren't able to stand up and be
true to yourself. Where is your voice? Why are you not shining
your light into the world?

Friday 29th

The Sun meets Jupiter today in your health and duties sector. These two energetic planets will help to make your day brighter and more optimistic. Come out into the light now and do what you do best. The efficient you is needed in the world right now.

Saturday 30th

Mercury goes retrograde tomorrow so use today to back up all your devices and double-check travel plans. As this occurs in your health and duties sector, be sure to keep to your schedule at all times and message ahead if you are going to be late. Be that forward-thinking Virgo now.

Sunday 31st

The Moon is now in your sign and you feel more like yourself. Mars gives you the drive you need to stay on task and get everything done. Long distance communications, over the phone or online, may fill your day. Stay busy and don't listen to Neptune's call.

FEBRUARY

....

Monday 1st

Venus spends her last day in your creative sector. It's crucial that you complete a creative project or make the first move on a love interest now. She moves this evening and will spend time teaching you to take care of your body. You're juggling your work and other duties.

Tuesday 2nd

The Moon is in your finance and value sector. This increases the need for you to check any imbalances with your health. Jupiter and the Sun continue to bless you with good fortune today. This could mean an increase or sudden windfall of money. Check your bank balance.

Wednesday 3rd

Mars and Venus are at odds today. You may witness power struggles between men and women, particularly at work. You're emotionally drawn to investigate this and will likely pull out a few hidden discrepancies. Your eagle eye for detail will not let anything pass you by.

Thursday 4th

The Moon makes difficult connections to the planets in your health and duties sector today. Getting angry and hostile will not help the problems. Mars and Uranus are triggered in your career sector and your emotions can be quite volatile. Bite your tongue if you have to, this energy will soon pass.

Friday 5th

Secrets and lies are being exposed now. This can make you feel powerful and in control. Mercury retrograde is discovering areas of deceit within your duties sector. Observe how people react but do not take it upon yourself to be judge and jury. Enjoy your own space when evening comes.

Saturday 6th

Venus meets Saturn today. There's a lot of planetary activity in your health and duties sector. Venus makes sure that Saturn isn't working you so hard that you forget to meet your own needs. Today could be filled with gym visits and mundane jobs to do, but this is not necessarily a bad thing. Getting ahead of your personal tasks can make it easier to relax later, and you can get a buzz out of feeling productive.

Sunday 7th

Your weekend is so full of chores and outings that you may resent having no time for yourself. Neptune is coaxing you away for quality downtime with your lover or your favourite TV show. Venus and Uranus make you indecisive and frustrated today. Try taking an hour to unwind and reconnect with yourself to be at your best.

Monday 8th

Mercury has nothing to say today as he is in the heat of the Sun. As Mercury is your ruler, you would be wise to do the same. Listen and observe what goes on around you, rather than charging in and taking over discussions. Keep your ears open for messages or information that you can use at a later date, or lessons which can help you to grow.

Tuesday 9th

You may experience some passive-aggressive behaviour coming from your love affairs or creative projects today. Mars connects to your emotions and makes you aware of this. Get armoured up and let this behaviour bounce off you rather than responding and getting dragged into unpleasantness. Neptune can throw his mist over you. You come away unfazed.

Wednesday 10th

The Moon meets Venus, Saturn and Jupiter. You are on an emotional roller-coaster at the moment. Free love, regulations and expansion cause you a tumultuous day. Mercury and Mars square off to confuse you even more. You may have to give in and go with the flow to save yourself being stressed. Try not to let it overwhelm you.

Thursday 11th

A New Moon occurs in your very busy sector of health and duties. This is your chance to review if your extra obligations are working or not, and to consider what to do moving forwards. The two luck-bringing planets, Venus and Jupiter, connect and give you emotional support. Mercury also butts in, mind that you say what you mean.

Friday 12th

The Moon dips into your relationship sector and gives you a break for a little while. You may begin the weekend in a total haze of otherworldliness. This probably means that vices such as alcohol are involved and you switch off totally. Enjoy drifting away but stay safe and with a tow rope attached.

Saturday 13th

Neptune wants you to continue spending your weekend in fantasy land. Indulge yourself and enjoy it. Perhaps you could spend the day with someone special watching your favourite films or, if alone, read a good book. Mercury retrograde meets Venus and asks that you are fit and healthy. If not, do something about it.

Sunday 14th

Mercury meets Jupiter. Today can be so full of chatter that you'll be glad for bedtime. However, by evening your mind is contemplating the unanswered questions of life and you cannot switch off and sleep. Turn your thoughts into something more solid and tangible. After a few days of dreaming, it's time to come back down to earth.

Monday 15th

Today you form plans on how to deal with your overload of mundane duties for other people. You know that you have to let something go now for the sake of your own health. It's difficult to do so as you don't like letting people down.

Tuesday 16th

You're halted in your progress to move on with a love affair or creative project. Step back and you will notice that this is a shout out to make more time for yourself. Venus is asking that you be a rebel and say no for a change.

Wednesday 17th

The Moon enters earthy territory which you are familiar with. You wish to get outside and be more hands-on. Gardening can be a new venture that satisfies this need. Be a good Virgo and research this prospect. A pleasant surprise awaits you when you see that this could really work for you.

Thursday 18th

The Sun enters your relationship sector today. This time will be almost surreal, and you may have to pinch yourself once or twice. You will see yourself projected through the eyes of another. The Moon meets Mars bringing your emotions close to the surface. Build or destroy is your choice.

Friday 19th

The energy today is frustrating for you. Mars and Venus are not speaking. She isn't happy with more plans for your time unless they're truly for you alone. Saturn and Uranus have a similar feel in the same areas. Do you pull back or blow up?

Saturday 20th

The Moon is in your career sector. You have a duty and a natural inclination to seek out information which is useful. Your leadership qualities are marked on how your enthusiasm lets you research relentlessly. Today, your mind is full of contrary ideas you need to sift through.

Sunday 21st

Your ruler Mercury goes direct. This is a relief as your health and duties sector has been very busy lately. Any rebellious thinking will now be pacified, and you can sweet-talk your way back into balance. The Moon's monthly visit to the point of fate has you filling your planner.

Monday 22nd

This morning the Moon enters your social sector. A nice connection to Uranus can mean that your wider friendship or working groups come up with fresh new thinking. A bright start to the week makes you happy if a little protective over your own innovative ideas. Own your inner genius.

Tuesday 23rd

You're more sensitive than usual today. The Moon connects to Neptune, who asks that you listen to your inner voice. Assistance from your relationships sector makes you feel nurtured. Someone here is taking care of your needs and offering protection. Take it and offer the same back.

Wednesday 24th

Mars gives you the energy you need to armour yourself up and be defensive. You may feel hurt and offended when trying to express yourself. Someone is likely jealous of you. Don't be afraid, state your case with honesty and compassion. Be brave.

Thursday 25th

Venus spends her final day in your health and duties sector. She leaves just as the Moon opposes all the other planets there. This can be confusing as you are pulled in all directions. Too many people are demanding your attention and you may just erupt into tears or anger.

Friday 26th

Venus is bringing love and harmony to your relationship sector. This is a soothing balm and you lap it up. The Moon in your hidden sector sits opposite and you are quite happy to be taken care of by someone special today. You aren't in the mood to initiate anything.

Saturday 27th

A beautiful Full Moon in your sign illuminates how you have been serving others and ignoring your own needs. You realise now that more time for introspection is required. This gives you an excuse to buy a new notebook and planner. Remember to schedule plenty of time for yourself.

Sunday 28th

A lot of earthy energy makes you feel perfectly at home today. You're more in control of your emotions. Use this energy to make solid, grounded plans which are attainable and will bring you security. Perhaps you find a money-making scheme. You're determined to see this through.

MARCH

· · · · · · · · · · · · · · · · ·

Monday 1st

Take pride in your home environment today. You have a sense that everything's in order and bringing you joy. Mercury, Jupiter and Saturn connect to your emotions and make you feel grown up and responsible with money. Your finances are looking healthy, don't take unnecessary risks.

Tuesday 2nd

This is a pleasant day. You have foresight and can see where you are heading this year. Look back at lessons and skills you've learned that you may wish to bring forward and use once more whilst learning something completely new. Harmony is achieved and you can relax.

Wednesday 3rd

The Moon enters your communications sector. Shrewd investigations help to unearth fine details you may have missed before. A lover or business partner will be your accomplice today as you surprise or shock people with your knowledge of foreign affairs. Just be careful not to show off about this.

Thursday 4th

You may come across some bitter words from a person in your busy health and duties sector. Someone doesn't like seeing you succeed. Take it with a pinch of salt, this will bother them more than you. It's your life, your dream and you can make it real.

Friday 5th

Mars is on the final degree of your travel sector. Now that you have formed the plans in your head, Mars will step up and give you the momentum to carry them out. However, his opposition to the Moon may give you doubts. A partner is having doubts too.

Saturday 6th

The Moon touches your family sector today. Here you are outgoing and fearless. Watch how you act because people are looking up to you. A nice connection to Mercury and Jupiter means that you have a lot to talk about with family members. Note who supports you.

Sunday 7th

Pleasant surprises light up your creative sector today. Venus is giving out ethereal vibes and offering you a sexy Sunday afternoon. Love and passion combine to make time spent with a loved one very special. You may plan future trips or a stunning garden together. Venus is happy about this.

Monday 8th

You do a lot of thinking today. Neptune connects to the Moon and gets you to see your way around a problem. This isn't serious, it's more likely to be how you go about initiating a new project. Let your partner offer their advice too. Two minds may be better than one.

Tuesday 9th

The Moon connects to both Pluto and Mars giving you the strength and energy to end something which no longer serves you. This can feel a little upsetting. It's absolutely necessary to make space for something bigger and better to come in and enhance your life.

Wednesday 10th

The Sun and Neptune meet up. The Sun will burn away any mist or fog that has been collecting around relationship issues. You can now clearly see a partner or situation for what they really are. It could be that your own projections have broken down and reality has set in.

Thursday 11th

Mercury is visited by the Moon and your mind will be busier than usual. Emotional attachments to issues in your health and duties sector will be reviewed. This may cause you some angst. Enjoy relationship time this evening and share your woes with a loved one.

Friday 12th

The urge to merge with a lover or with a higher source fills you with longing. You need to follow a path but as yet don't know where to start. Forever the romantic in relationships, you see this as a mission or quest and understand that you are blessed to have it.

Saturday 13th

A New Moon in your relationship sector has come at just the right time for you. Take advantage of this to set goals and intentions regarding important relationships, your calling and higher self. Neptune asks that you find your inner compass which will point to your true north.

Sunday 14th

A surreal day is brought to you by Venus and Neptune meeting up. You may feel like you've eaten a something strange and entered a fantasy land. Your senses are heightened and everything is felt acutely. Tune in to divine messages and dreams today. What will you learn?

Monday 15th

A fiery Moon brings you back down to earth and ready to start a new week. Your head is full of schemes waiting to be activated. You may have too many plans. Take a look and see which are pipe dreams and which are achievable.

Tuesday 16th

Mercury is now in your relationship sector. Expect conversations with loved ones to be deep and meaningful, if a little surreal. It's time to ground your plans under this Moon in your travel sector. Examine how valuable they are to you and put in the required effort.

Wednesday 17th

You may get a moment of genius thinking where you either solve a problem or think up a way to earn money. Think this through carefully, Saturn is watching and isn't so sure you have the time or energy to commit. Define your own limits and don't over-stretch yourself.

Thursday 18th

It's possible that you come up against an authority figure who isn't keen on your plans. It may be that you need to do more research about legalities or by-laws. However, this doesn't stop you dreaming and clearing the decks. Your lover is willing to help you with this.

Friday 19th

The Moon now meets Mars in your career sector. Mercury is squaring off with the Moon too. This energy can bring about arguments in the workplace. Someone doesn't agree with your points of view. Keep your cool and take time to respond to anyone acting like a bully.

Saturday 20th

The Sun moves into Aries which means that it's the Spring Equinox. Your intimacy sector is highlighted here. Take time to pause and reflect on your plans before the longer days and warmer weather compels you into action. You know the way forward, but think it through first.

Sunday 21st

As Venus moves into your intimacy sector she becomes the warrior goddess. This shift may not sit very well with you at first. Your loving support has now become rather pushy. Do not worry, once you feel the compassionate warrior rise, you will appreciate that strength and love can be combined.

Monday 22nd

You rally the troops and get busy with your social groups. Networking with online friends or interest groups makes you protective about your plans. Your ruler, Mercury, helps you to break through some barriers to get the information you need. These are all steps to aid your self-growth.

Tuesday 23rd

Do not let anyone put you off finding you path. You may come up against opposition or jealousy in your creative sector. Take baby steps and you will not fail. Keep dreaming but remain realistic. Your shadow-side may be unrealistic and changeable now, keep your eye on the goal.

Wednesday 24th

It may be difficult to find your voice today. The Moon in your hidden sector makes you turn inward for fear of upsetting others. Mercury and Mars squaring off signify this too. Venus and the Sun are making soft connections asking you to take care of your own needs.

Thursday 25th

The best thing to do today is to go within and listen to what your inner child says. It may want to stand up and be counted but you must pay attention to why it thinks it needs to do this. Deep introspection is possible now. A loving partner might help.

Friday 26th

This morning the Moon lands back in your sign and you feel more balanced. Your sudden shift of mood gets you activated, and your inner child is pleased. Root out your stationery drawer or put your books in alphabetical order. Mars in your career sector makes you more assertive.

Saturday 27th

Tension from poor Moon connections fills your head with unnecessary worries. You're driven but dreamy, chatty but prefer solitude. Pluto helps you regain self-control and fix on a mood. It's a good time to declutter and say goodbye to projects that aren't going anywhere. Let things go now.

Sunday 28th

A Full Moon occurring in your finances and worth sector illuminates all that you hold value in. Perhaps it was hard to get rid of pre-loved items. However, this will teach you what's important to you and what's taking up space. Remember to be kind to yourself too.

Monday 29th

Today is more uplifting and you're determined to make an impression on someone. You may be entertaining at home or simply enjoying the clean space you now have. Mars helps you to plough through the day in good spirits. Saturn and Jupiter are watching you with pride.

Tuesday 30th

The Moon shifts into your communications sector and your mind is sharp and inquisitive. You may startle someone with your knowledge of a secret or two. Mercury and Neptune meet up and your dreams may be vivid tonight. Sharing dreams and visions with a loved one can be a fun experience.

Wednesday 31st

You have the strangest way of beguiling someone today. Conversations can border on the taboo but are received well. Just remember to note when you're pushing a boundary and pull back if you must. A lover or special person will enjoy the deep discussions you have today.

APRIL

. . . .

Thursday 1st

You're more outgoing today and concern yourself with family and home. Think of a general rallying his troops as this is what your energy is like now. Optimism and good cheer help to keep your family interactions lively. A youngster may be asking for your words of wisdom.

Friday 2nd

The Moon makes a lot of helpful connections today. You can truly lead the way and be an inspiration to those around you. However, your work environment may drain you and give pressure. Your ruler, Mercury, is talking to Pluto. Love, romance and expression are up for review and require small tweaks.

Saturday 3rd

Mercury is now at odds with the Moon. You may be emotionally stuck today. Is there something you wish to discuss with a lover or special person? Mercury is about to leave your relationship sector, making it crucial that you say what's on your mind now.

Sunday 4th

Venus as the warrior goddess in your intimacy sector is touching on subjects you'd rather not know about. Compassion for others must first be practised on yourself. Go deep within you to see what needs attention. Mercury now joins the mission of excavating your shared finances and secrets.

. . . .

Monday 5th

Today you may feel a little restricted in your expressions. You will have to toe the line or take back control. The Moon and Mercury help you to do this with considered assertiveness. There will be no need for anyone to get hurt. Revolutionise the way you respond.

Tuesday 6th

Sort through your jobs list and come up with a new way of getting things done. When the Moon meets Saturn you feel blocked but need to break your way through this wall. Take out your frustrations on physical exercise. Male and female relationships unite to solve a problem today.

Wednesday 7th

As the Moon meets Jupiter today, it's possible that you come up against the law or other authority. This combined energy can also make any existing mood you are in much larger. If this is negative, remember that this will pass soon. Concentrate on being efficient at work.

Thursday 8th

The Moon slips into your relationship sector today. This may come as a welcome respite from recent tensions. Alternatively, it will highlight your shadow side as your partner may reflect your mood back at you. You may feel stuck and have a momentary crisis of conscience.

Friday 9th

Dreamy Neptune meets the Moon today and you're asked to employ patience. You may feel irritation at work and an urgency to complete something but relax and breathe. Nothing will get done if you rush and make mistakes. Allow yourself to pause before taking the next steps required.

Saturday 10th

The weekend is here and you're inclined to do some digging around in your intimacy sector. Mercury reminds you to respect boundaries as you investigate touchy subjects. A connection between Venus and Jupiter helps you to be kind, considerate and get what you need without upsetting anyone. Be a compassionate warrior today.

Sunday 11th

The Moon meets your ruler and together they have a heart to heat. Your mind will be doing overtime and you overthink your emotions. Don't get yourself in a tangle. Use your ruler's help to think and communicate clearly. Deep emotions can surface and be expressed.

Monday 12th

There's a New Moon in your intimacy sector. This area also deals with life's mysteries and shared finances. As the Moon meets Venus, money is certainly the theme for you today and the next six months. Check your taxes, shared investments and any money owing. Aim for a clean slate.

Tuesday 13th

As the Moon shifts, it enters your travel sector and meets
Uranus. Expect the unexpected today. It's likely that you
spend too much on an impulse buy and regret it later. You're
yearning for a bit of the good life, try dining out tonight.

Wednesday 14th

Venus is at the last degree of your intimacy sector. It's critical
now that you check any finances you hold with another. A
close relationship may have been strengthened by Venus but
now she asks that you carry on the lesson you have learned.
You can do this.

Thursday 15th

Money continues to be a concern. Venus moves into her own
sign and will tend to your bank account. You may find that
you're eating out or making trips more now. The Moon is in
your career sector and your mind is overloaded with ideas
and research.

Friday 16th

Where is your career going? You may be asking yourself
that today. If you have any queries or would like to discuss
advancement, now is the time. You are respected for your
inquisitive mind which covers all bases. Every detail is
examined and you leave nothing out. This is your strength.

Saturday 17th

This is a very busy weekend where your mind goes into
overdrive. The energy is amped up to the maximum as your
thought processes rush ahead and consider all angles of
a problem. You are pioneering a new course of action for
yourself. Schedule time for fun this weekend too.

Sunday 18th

Today you feel safe and protected. Your friendship groups surround you and there are social occasions that you just cannot say no to. Mercury is silent now and asks that you spend time with your groups and unwind. Venus and Uranus support this and allow you to enjoy yourself.

Monday 19th

Both the Sun and Mercury move into your travel sector today. This is great news as you can now think about trips and holidays you would like to make this year. An exotic location with delicious food attracts you. Get out the travel brochures and browse where you would like to go.

Tuesday 20th

Don't be distracted by nay-sayers today. You are more sensitive than usual to criticism and if you aren't careful you can bite back. Be determined not to compromise your own beliefs and values now. Stand up for yourself, or retreat and don't get involved.

Wednesday 21st

The Moon in your hidden sector makes you feel irritable. It's possible that your inner child surfaces and you find yourself sulking. You're resentful towards someone who appears to be laughing at you today. Uranus is connecting to the Moon, do not let his energy erupt and cause problems.

Thursday 22nd

This afternoon you're back in control and feel like yourself again. Your mood lifts and you become cheerful and optimistic again. Mars is at the final degree of your career sector. He will give you an extra boost to finish a project today. You may also be extra chatty.

Friday 23rd

With the Moon in your own sign, you get things around you in order. Today you are the super-efficient Virgo you are known as and loved for. Venus and Uranus meet, meaning that you can inject exciting energy into your travel plans. You may burst with excitement. Start making notes and dates.

Saturday 24th

Neptune calls you today but you have no time for unnecessary dreaming. Your lover or shadow side may be asking for attention. Be careful that your mouth doesn't run away with you this evening. Your head may be too full of ideas and something may have to go.

Sunday 25th

Mercury and Venus meet in your travel sector. Your mind wants to know what your heart wants in this area. Mercury asks you to consider a course of higher education or learning a new language. Venus wants to eat her way around the world. Be sensible about what you plan.

Monday 26th

You have so much energy today that you find yourself doing a lot of favours for others. Are you feeling protective of someone? Do they need this or are you smothering them? You may not be able to see where you are being pushy. Do not over-react to criticism.

Tuesday 27th

A Full Moon in your communications sector may reveal secrets, lies or painful truths. This is a very intense day and you must learn not to take things too personally. The Moon sits opposite Venus, Mercury and Uranus in your travel sector. Let your excitement subside, just for today.

Wednesday 28th

Pluto, the planet of permanent change turns retrograde today. This occurs in your creative sector. Self-expression or getting your own way will be difficult now. You will discover that something will come to an end during this cycle. Do this yourself before Pluto does it for you.

Thursday 29th

The Moon shifts into your family sector and you are feeling subdued. The tension of the Full Moon is still lingering. You find that you look back to the past and reminisce about adventures that you had. What skills did you learn that you can use again now?

Friday 30th

The Sun meets Uranus today. This is highly volatile energy and can disrupt the status quo. Be warned that something in your travel sector is highlighted. You may be running for cover or jumping up and down after discovering something brand new and innovative. This will keep you awake tonight.

MAY

· · · · · · · · · · · · · · · · · ·

Saturday 1st

That highly charged energy is still available to you. Keep your emotions out of the way and look at what it is that you really want to change. The Moon makes no contacts so today is all about self, ego and how you go after what you desire. Act now for best effect.

Sunday 2nd

Today, the Moon meets newly retrograde Pluto. You know in your heart what needs to change or be brought to an end. Listen to your inner voice as Mercury is involved here too. Your recent dreams and imaginings will give you a clue. This evening you wish to share the love.

Monday 3rd

Saturn the teacher planet has a lesson for you. His job is to teach you about your responsibilities and grown-up duties. As he sits in your duties sector his lesson will come to you loud and clear. This might rattle your travel plans a little.

Tuesday 4th

Mercury enters your career sector today. This is his home sign so he's ready to network like crazy. Your mind will be busier than usual and you may find that you meet many new connections now. Thought processes will enter and leave your head quickly so write everything down.

Wednesday 5th

Another elder, teacher or person in authority brings you a lesson today. Jupiter meets the Moon and asks you to seek the answer in the wider world. You should look at your eating habits today too as Jupiter can expand your waistline. This evening, your relationship sector draws you to connect.

Thursday 6th

A floaty Moon makes relating to a lover easy today. The meeting with Neptune can turn things on its head and you look at life through the eyes of another. Jupiter sits at the last degree of your duties sector and asks if you have really done all you can for others recently.

Friday 7th

Get ready for an active weekend as the Moon moves into your intimacy sector. This could mean that you get to know someone on a deeper level. Venus and Pluto help you to transform an existing love affair into gold. Remember that Pluto is retrograde and needs to see a change.

Saturday 8th

Did you dig too deeply with a lover? Mars is getting defensive in your hidden sector. You must be willing to share back if you desire to know another's secrets. Venus and Jupiter are arguing about personal love and free love. Be responsible and respectful at all times.

Sunday 9th

The Moon enters your travel sector just as Venus leaves it. She has laid the ground for you to grow your plans. You must now tend the garden and bring your plans to fruition. In your career sector, she will be the Lady Boss and enhance your money-making schemes.

Monday 10th

Today you may have feelings that are under the surface and waiting to blow up like a volcano. You do your best to keep them hidden but there are many triggers and you feel vulnerable. Lie low if you can, keep your head down and distract yourself.

Tuesday 11th

A New Moon in your travel sector gives you the chance to set intentions. With your ruler joining the point of fate today, you would be wise you use this energy wisely. Make arrangements to tend to your plans and help them thrive. In turn, you will take joy from them.

Wednesday 12th

The Moon now meets Venus and you feel content. Something in you has changed and you're resolved to seeing your goals for this year, and beyond, manifested. Inner stirrings from deep within you rumble around. Play with these for a while, they may be golden nuggets for you to use.

Thursday 13th

Jupiter enters your relationship sector. This is a special time for you. Despite a retrograde period, the planet of luck will add joy, optimism, truth and expansion. Expect your important relationships to grow over the next 12 months. Listen to your self-talk today. What does it say about you?

Friday 14th

Today you must take time to see where you may have been drawn into an illusion. The Moon squares off with Neptune who likes to cast a mist over everything. Be careful not to get drawn into foggy or unrealistic thinking. Take a sideways glance at someone now.

Saturday 15th

The Moon dips into your social sector but today you feel vulnerable. Take the day off and do what feeds your soul. Enjoy treating yourself to your favourite foods and time with a good book or tv show. Self-care is needed now so retreat just for the day. Nurture yourself.

Sunday 16th

You are super-sensitive today, and tears of anger may not be too far away. Mars and the Moon meet up and you feel defensive. Make sure that you're seeing a person or situation clearly as you may have been hoodwinked by someone. Be careful who you take into your confidence now.

Monday 17th

Your courage returns slowly and you feel up to starting a new week. Egos may have been wounded over the weekend, yours included. Stand up and be counted today. The Moon is in your hidden sector and gives you inner strength. You are good enough, show them that.

Tuesday 18th

Be brave enough to face an elder or teacher today. They are not out to get you but want to guide you in the right direction. Feelings may be tender and raw so be willing to listen and also speak your own truth. This will not be as bad as you think.

Wednesday 19th

Take things slowly today. You're coming back to your optimum self and don't need to be knocked back again. Another person in authority may oppose you, listen and learn. There's wisdom here for you to access. Pay heed to good advice now.

Thursday 20th

The Sun moves into your career sector. Now is the time for you to stand up and shine. You may be showcasing your talents over the next month. Nervous tension is filling you and making you restless. Do some filing or paperwork to settle your mind on a task.

Friday 21st

When the Moon is in your sign, you may see yourself at your best. Neptune is attempting to bewitch you away into idealistic thinking, but you know better. Your keen eye for detail will see through Neptune's call. You may need to be aggressive to get things done today.

Saturday 22nd

You have a job to rationalise your thinking today. Neptune is determined to take you to fantasy land and is now squaring off with your ruler. Follow Mercury's lead and keep your mind occupied with logic. You find that balancing your finances helps you to think more clearly.

Sunday 23rd

Saturn turns retrograde today. This will be a tricky time in your health and duties sector. Don't start anything new or take on extra duties or you will get burnt out. You are about to experience a four-month lesson on boundaries and responsibilities. Be there for others but put yourself first.

Monday 24th

Shrewd thinking can solve a problem today. Interactions with others can be secretive or you may be given only half of the information you need. Any study you do at this time will be focused and intense. It may be hard to switch off at the end of the day.

Tuesday 25th

The Moon connects to newly retrograde Saturn. You may be feeling the first effects of this. If your conversations are being misunderstood, make sure you repeat your words until everyone is clear. It's possible that you see some passive-aggression coming towards you from your relationships.

Wednesday 26th

Today there's a Full Moon in your family sector. This fiery Moon will illuminate all that has transpired in this area for the last six months. How has your family life been an adventure? Have you needed to seek out the truth or justice? How have you nurtured each other?

Thursday 27th

Venus and Mercury both face opposition from the Moon today. As they are both in your career sector you may expect a setback in the workplace. An idea or project may be scrapped now as it has been proven to have no value. Never mind, clear the ground for something new.

Friday 28th

Mercury goes retrograde tomorrow so today is best used in preparation. Back up all your devices, double-check travel plans and ensure clear communications. This will happen in your career sector so be mindful that your workload will become stressful for the next three weeks.

Saturday 29th

As Mercury goes retrograde today he meets Venus. He hands over the reins to a more compassionate, harmonising planet to help you get through this. The message here is to always act with love even if you have to fire someone during this period. Look for older females to advise you.

Sunday 30th

Today there's gentle energy to give you some breathing space. The Moon edges into your health and duties sector. You can take a look at what you do here. How much do you serve others? Are you getting the same back? Are there any duties you can let go of now?

Monday 31st

The Moon meets Saturn. He will ask if you have healthy boundaries. He will also ask when you last got a health check-up. Do yourself a favour and tune into what your body needs. You may wish to use this Saturn retrograde to start an exercise regime.

JUNE
....

Tuesday 1st

Your special relationships come into focus now. You may well be sitting together and reaching out towards your future selves. Emotions may reach new levels between you as the Moon meets Jupiter. Exploring the width and breadth of this relationship will bring you and your partner joy.

Wednesday 2nd

Venus makes her way into your social sector today. Here she will be the ultimate nurturer or the intuitive Goddess. It's important that your female friendships are strong and you respect the wise words of feminine wisdom. You may see a pregnancy within your group now.

Thursday 3rd

The Moon meets Neptune making you drift off-task and into fantasy. Your dreams are important but remember to stay focused in your daily life. Partnerships can border on being unrealistic but can also prove that dreaming together means staying together. Mercury and Venus need you to keep it real.

Friday 4th

Your mood turns towards deeper issues and solving problems. However, you may find that you're creating problems where there were none. Venus and Jupiter make a nice connection between lovers and friends. Involve your partner in your friendship groups and increase the potential depth of this relationship.

Saturday 5th

The energy today suggests that there are control issues around. You may be standing in the middle of a conflict between men and women or friends and lovers. Don't say anything you don't mean as Mercury and Neptune are squaring off and making a big misunderstanding possible.

Sunday 6th

This morning the Moon slips into your travel sector and you desire to taste delights from foreign lands. You have an urge to connect with the exotic. A trip to a global restaurant would be a good thing to do today. Sample what other cultures have to offer. Think of it as research.

Monday 7th

The Moon meets up with volatile Uranus. Expect the sudden and unexpected but take it all in your stride. This energy can also mean that you are restless and wish to get out there and wander. Do something different, even if it's just in what you wear.

Tuesday 8th

Your mind is in overdrive once more. You are driven and get things done today. Pluto connects and you may get an idea of what his retrograde is asking you to change. Watch out that you don't upset an authority today as you may get more than you bargained for.

Wednesday 9th

The Moon joins the point of fate and you find yourself wondering about where your career is going. What would you like to leave behind as your legacy? A connection to Saturn asks that you consider all of your obligations, not just your work ones.

Thursday 10th

Today there's a New Moon in your career sector. This is a tricky one as it also connects to Mercury in retrograde. Be very careful how you voice your intentions now as they will be misunderstood. Keep them to yourself for now until the retrograde is over and then implement them.

Friday 11th

Your ruler has nothing to say today as he's in the heat of the Sun. Listen very carefully to your inner voice. You may find it hard to distinguish from the devil and angel on each shoulder. Mars enters your hidden sector. Your private life will become more active.

Saturday 12th

Use today for spending time with friends, especially your female ones. The Moon meets Venus making the energy very feminine. Are you the nurturer in your wider groups? If not, look at who is and honour the job they selflessly do. You may get a nice surprise today.

Sunday 13th

Your hidden sector is touched by the Moon today. Emotions need a bit more courage to be expressed. Mars is here and he will help to strengthen your personal weaknesses and turn them into something worth celebrating. Stay in control and don't be tempted to self-medicate and switch off.

Monday 14th

Today you might be touchy and vulnerable. You desire to have your own space in order to rant. Use Mars' energy to do something productive. If you feel you're being victimised, simply withdraw and don't respond. Let the energy pass over you, as the Moon will soon shift into different waters.

Tuesday 15th

Keep your head today. Saturn and Uranus are squaring off. The teacher and the disruptor will not give you an easy time today. You'll find that people demand your attention, your time and your energy. There will be very little left over for you by the end of the day.

Wednesday 16th

There is time to be yourself today. The Moon is in your sign and you can be your perfect self. An opposition to Jupiter in your relationship sector can make you feel that you should be attending to another. Let them bring the joy your way.

Thursday 17th

You can be unconventional. Sticking to your schedule is commendable but you feel like rebelling. Your friendship groups and travel interests draw you outside of yourself for some unusual activities. Personal relationships are too intangible for you to spend time with now, you prefer more grounding interactions.

Friday 18th

Aim for balance and harmony. You spend part of the day tidying, decluttering and beautifying your home. Mars gives you the energy and Pluto likes to see how you recycle and reuse stuff in your home. When your home environment is clear, so are your mind and emotions.

Saturday 19th

A misunderstanding within your wider groups causes you
some concern. This may be on social media where you find
that someone has spoken out of line. Your instinct is to
protect the group from outsiders. Clear thinking and unbiased
decisions are needed, and you may be the one passing the
judgement.

Sunday 20th

There's intrigue going on and you're determined to root it
out. You may witness jealousy and spite coming from your
creative sector. This may be coming from you, check in with
yourself first. Mars in your hidden sector brings up something
uncomfortable for you to deal with.

Monday 21st

Today is the Summer Solstice. The Sun moves into your social
sector, fun and laughter will enhance your friendship circles.
Jupiter turns retrograde in your relationship sector, you must
evaluate the joy personal relationships are bringing you. You
may see things you don't particularly like now.

Tuesday 22nd

Mercury finally turns direct. You're good to go now if you
have delayed any travel or career moves. The Moon squares
off against Jupiter and you may get the first effect of this
retrograde. Is your personal relationship fulfilling? You're
emotionally ready to look at this objectively.

Wednesday 23rd

Your heart and mind are not in sync today. This can make it difficult to see that there are control issues going on between your social and creative sectors. Make time to be with friends but remember that you're an individual and have your own passions too.

Thursday 24th

A Full Moon in your creative sector shows the culmination of a project or love affair that you began six months ago. What have you worked hard for? What has taken you many small steps to climb? Take off the rose-coloured spectacles and take a good look from the top of this mountain.

Friday 25th

Dreamy Neptune turns retrograde now. Your relationship sector is getting another wake-up call. Neptune asks that you consider the meaning of sacrifice and surrender. Have you lost yourself for the sake of another? Have you compromised too much? Pause and listen to your inner voice.

Saturday 26th

The Moon meets Pluto in your creative sector. You will find that you're unable to say what is on your mind. It's difficult for you to express who you really are as you dumb yourself down too much. Male versus female power struggles will be evident now.

Sunday 27th

Today you feel the need to do mundane things such as DIY or paying visits to family members. Your heart isn't in it, but it stops you thinking about deeper issues. You're irritable and wish to rebel but today you focus on keeping the peace.

Monday 28th

Venus is now in your hidden sector. She will help you realise your own self-worth and teach you to love your shadow parts. Your divine essence is shut away and the time has come to let it loose, warts and all. Offer the hand of peace to a loved one this evening.

Tuesday 29th

A crisis of conscience can chip away at you today. Are you being true to yourself or being subtly manipulated by another? This is a good day to take a step back and have a talk with yourself. Dreamy, unrealistic thinking needs to stop now. You may be projecting onto a partner.

Wednesday 30th

As the Moon meets Neptune, you're emotionally charged and not sure how to proceed. This monthly meeting asks that you pause and find your inner compass. Make sure that what you're doing is aligned with your true self. If it isn't, let it go.

JULY

· · · · · · · · · · · · · · · · ·

Thursday 1st

A helping hand from Venus gets you looking deeply at the mysteries of life. Remembering what you desire gives you more optimism today. You will have that devil on your shoulder telling you all the reasons you should not be happy, don't listen to it.

Friday 2nd

Your inner voice keeps your mind busy today. Mercury is busy filling you with ideas on how to progress at work. Mars gives you the drive to be proficient and Saturn watches every move you make. You impress the right people. Well done, this is a good day for you.

Saturday 3rd

You re-ignite your passion to experience other cultures. It's not an easy task to discuss this with a lover today as they may be trying to bend your will. If this is something you wish to do alone, then say so. Speak up now and make your partner aware.

Sunday 4th

Difficult planetary energy makes you emotionally unstable. The Moon meets Uranus and although you try to keep anger at bay, it may erupt suddenly. You feel restricted by your responsibilities. This also has the effect of making you feel that you aren't worthy. Relax, this will soon pass.

Monday 5th

Deep feelings are warmed up by the Sun in your hidden sector today. Uranus connects and helps you to excavate these without cause for concern. Your inner compass is also triggered and you know which direction you should be heading. Change is coming, don't be afraid of it.

Tuesday 6th

As the Moon moves into your career sector, you switch your focus to your job. You have many tasks to do and this may feel overwhelming at first. When you've found your groove, these tasks become a helpful way to get through the day without distractions.

Wednesday 7th

A conflict with a person in authority may leave you feeling undermined but Venus helps you to find your centre again and carry on. This was a trigger to show you what needs healing next. With both Venus and Mars in your hidden sector, you will be able to stand up for yourself now.

Thursday 8th

Neptune does his best to distract you today, but you manage to stay on task. As the Moon meets your ruler, your mind becomes very busy solving problems in the workplace. Your head and heart are aligned and you work methodically without interruption from dreamy Neptune.

Friday 9th

Today you want to let off steam with your social groups. A night out could be just the place to rant, cry or laugh within a safe environment. Online groups can also be a great space to do this. You may surprise yourself and come up with new ways of nurturing yourself.

Saturday 10th

A New Moon in your social sector allows you to set goals and intentions regarding mothering, nurturing, and looking after your friendships. You feel protective of your closest friends and wish to feel the same from them. What feeds your soul? Which friends do you admire most?

Sunday 11th

The Moon dips into your hidden sector and you may wish to be alone. Give yourself time to contemplate old wounds and triggers which have surfaced recently. You must find different coping mechanisms as the ones you've used since childhood are no longer efficient. Listen to an elder today.

Monday 12th

Venus and Mars are getting close in your hidden sector. The Moon meets them both today. Your emotions are triggered by compassion for yourself and enormous courage. Mercury, now in your social sector, helps you to be outspoken and to laugh. You need more of this.

Tuesday 13th

Mars and Venus, the celestial lovers, meet up today. Make the most of this important energy to align all parts of yourself. As these are in your hidden sector you will feel protected and loved. Personal strength, courage and compassion are there for you to access now.

Wednesday 14th

As Mars and Venus continue their secret date, the Moon in your sign connects to Uranus. Sudden revelations from within you will show the effect of the lovers meeting. You will feel more self-aware, and brave enough to show up as you truly are and not a faint copy.

Thursday 15th

Today you may clearly see how much you've been projecting your ideals in personal relationships. The Sun and Moon both connect to Neptune and the fog disappears. What you see in front of you now is your true self. Don't lose sight of this. Don't let ego get in the way.

Friday 16th

There's too much going on in your social sector today. It's possible that you have double booked and now have to choose which appointment to keep. Do not be thrown off balance, select your social interactions by order of priority. You cannot fit everything in.

Saturday 17th

Listen to your inner voice today as Venus and Mars are speaking to you. There's a need for you to be assertive and firm with someone, but you must do it with total compassion. Pluto is involved now so look to your creative sector for a clue.

Sunday 18th

An intense day for you as the Moon enters your communications sector. You must speak directly to someone but come across as cruel. This is because you can see right through falsity. Uranus connects so prepare for tantrums. Practice being the compassionate warrior today. You will be impressive.

Monday 19th

It's possible for you to get a glimpse through the eyes of someone else, today. If you change your perspective, you're more likely to see a situation in a whole new way. This will involve your close relationships which are already having a shake-up. Be kind.

Tuesday 20th

Set new boundaries or rebuild old ones. You may need to mentor a youngster in the family or get advice for yourself. Mercury and Uranus connect to ensure that communication is loving and nurturing. Uranus may show you a different approach to getting things done more easily. You'll be surprised.

Wednesday 21st

Venus and Mars are here again to see if you're practising being firm and loving. They are pleased with you. You have handled a situation which required just that, and you did it well. Spend the last hours of the day seeing to your mundane duties.

Thursday 22nd

Venus now enters your sign. Watch how your self-worth increases with her here. The Sun moves into your hidden sector and shines on parts you may wish to keep secret. This is a good time to heal and energise your deepest issues. There is a big shift happening. Watch as you rise.

Friday 23rd

You may wish to look at all your creative projects, including love affairs now. The Moon meets Pluto and if that change hasn't been made, it will be out of your hands soon. If something has been on the back-burner for too long, you might consider scrapping it to make space for something new.

Saturday 24th

A Full Moon lights up your health and duties sector today. Take a very good look at where you have neglected your own health. You may be doing too much for others and forgetting that you need to check in with yourself too. Be your own guru now.

Sunday 25th

This can be a difficult day. Your ruler is opposing the planet asking for change. Mercury does Pluto's bidding so take another look at what needs to be lovingly removed from your life. You will feel a huge resistance to this and will want to retreat and hide.

Monday 26th

Your personal relationships are highlighted by the Moon for the next few days. Venus sits opposite in your own sign reminding you to put yourself first. This isn't easy for you, you feel guilty for doing so. Jupiter connects to enhance any mood you are already in.

. . . .

Tuesday 27th

Neptune and Uranus connect to the Moon and make it a dreamy but unstable time. You have fallen into wishful thinking in order to avoid a necessary change. If you sit with yourself for long enough and listen to your inner voice, you'll find a way of doing this kindly.

Wednesday 28th

Mercury enters your hidden sector now. He's the master of rooting around and digging up gold in the deepest part of your psyche. As your ruler, he will communicate this to you via your dreams. The Moon slips into your intimacy sector and connects to Mercury. Pay attention to your dreams tonight.

Thursday 29th

You have formidable back-up entering your sign now. Mars marches in and will fill you with determination to stand up and be counted. You will be energised and driven. He immediately opposes Jupiter. You may already see yourself holding your own today. Well done.

Friday 30th

This evening why not treat yourself to an exotic dinner and refresh your taste for other cultures. The Moon enters your travel sector and you may wish to get away. Combine a little luxury and your passion for travel by eating well or watching a documentary about foreign lands.

Saturday 31st

You can be quite stubborn today. Your ego is telling you to do what it takes to satisfy any urges you may have. This can involve food, sex or spending money. If a hedonistic Saturday is really what you want, then go ahead. Let your hair down but stay safe at all times.

AUGUST

· · · · · · · · · · · · · · · · · ·

Sunday 1st

You're in an upbeat and outgoing mood today. A lover or special person will be pleasantly surprised by the attention they receive from you. A spontaneous activity or day trip will be fun. Mercury is quiet, but he knows that you're always listening to your inner voice.

Monday 2nd

The working week begins and may dampen your high spirits. The Sun in your hidden sector opposes Saturn. It's possible that you get a trigger or two relating to your service to other people. Mars and Jupiter will make your mood bigger than it need be. This will soon pass.

Tuesday 3rd

Put everything into your work today. Your attention to detail is appreciated by those around you. On a personal level, you're more comfortable with the Sun and Mercury shaking up your private thoughts. This is a healing that only a Virgo will understand.

Wednesday 4th

Be very careful that your mouth doesn't run away with you today. Mercury is squaring off with Uranus and this unpredictable energy can mean that you reveal secrets. You may also get something off your chest. This is a first step to remedying issues which may have been causing you some grief.

Thursday 5th

Today you feel the need to be protected to protect others.
Your friendship groups can be a great source of comfort. If
you're still needing to rant or let off steam, this is the place
to do it. Your online friends are safer still. Just don't be a
keyboard warrior.

Friday 6th

Venus in your sign, connecting to the Moon in a helpful way.
Self-care is essential today as others may be pushing your
boundaries. You're at the limits of your patience and very close
to erupting. However, softer energy from Neptune and Venus
help you do this responsibly.

Saturday 7th

This morning the Moon joins the other planets in your hidden
sector. You go from feeling vulnerable to self-righteous.
There's no point trying to justify your words and emotions to
someone who will not listen. The Sun and Uranus are at odds
and ego issues can cause trouble.

Sunday 8th

A New Moon in your hidden sector brings you strength and
a resolution to make yourself heard. No more being the
scapegoat, no more dumbing yourself down. You have feelings
and you're going to make sure you express them. This may
upset an elder but that is not your problem.

Monday 9th

The Moon flies by Mercury and you know that your heart and mind are in a true partnership now. As the Moon opposes Jupiter in your health and duties sector, you want to defy any authority figures who have been preventing your growth. Watch out for conflict that arises here.

Tuesday 10th

Today the Moon in your sign lets you make heart-based decisions for yourself. A connection with Mars brings out your strength and determination to do the right thing. Venus and Neptune are in opposition today. Venus tells you to always put yourself first despite what a lover may say.

Wednesday 11th

The Moon and Venus have a ladies' night. They discuss all the ways you can take care of yourself, raise your self-esteem and ask for what you desire. Mercury is at the final degree of your entire chart. It's crucial that your inner voice makes you listen today.

Thursday 12th

Your ruler, Mercury, is back home. Feel the pace of your communications pick up now. He will give you the ability to express yourself well. You may wish to grab a new notebook and make a plan of action. What would you like to learn? What would you like to change?

Friday 13th

The Moon in your finances and value sector squares off with Pluto, the lord of change. You may begin to feel an emotional tug towards material goods you must let go of. Remember that for you, a clean and tidy house gives you a better frame of mind.

Saturday 14th

This is a good weekend to get active. Mars and Mercury make a great connection to the Moon in your communications sector. Check in with friends and family you may have been neglecting. Get involved in deep, intense discussions about life's mysteries. Have fun with siblings and burn the midnight oil.

Sunday 15th

You may rattle a few nerves today as the intense Moon opposes Uranus. There are people in your travel sector, including teachers and religious leaders, whose ideas conflict with yours. Challenging the status quo is a part of your growth but do it with love and compassion.

Monday 16th

Venus waves goodbye to your sign and slips into your finances and value sector. This is still good news. Venus can enhance your bank balance and help beautify your home and environment. Family interactions may be tricky today. Arguments are possible if you speak without thinking. Practice the pause.

Tuesday 17th

A helpful connection between the Moon and the Sun allows some healing to take place. Conversations with family can bring up old emotions. Triggers are ready to be released now. What served you as protection when a child is no longer valid or useful. Big steps can be taken today.

Wednesday 18th

The Moon shifts gear and enters your creative sector. This may feel like a drag or an impossible task. Self-expression, children and falling in love are all things you take too seriously. Learn to laugh more. Remember your inner child and practise unfiltered speech for fun.

Thursday 19th

The Earth may move for you today, Uranus turns retrograde. This is a lively day with a lot of activity. Mercury meets Mars so be warned that this energy can be argumentative or animated. Think of a fast-paced ball game and this is what your conversations will be like.

Friday 20th

As the Moon shifts into your health and duties sector, you feel the urge to get all your chores done before the weekend. Don't strain yourself, keep back some energy for yourself. The Moon meets Saturn and this energy has you being self-disciplined. Try to have some fun this evening.

Saturday 21st

You're outgoing and altruistic today but don't fall back on old habits and allow yourself to be used. The Moon is at odds with newly retrograde Uranus and you may feel the energy as irritability or restlessness. The only person preventing you from enjoying the weekend is you.

Sunday 22nd

There's a Full Moon today at the final degree of your health and duties sector. This will highlight what you have done for others and what you have omitted to do for yourself. This Moon wants to share the love but not at the expense of your own health. The Sun enters your sign, happy birthday!

Monday 23rd

Relationships need your attention today. Something is niggling away deep inside you and you need to discuss this with a partner. The Moon connects to both Uranus and Mars so don't expect today to go smoothly. At best, you can shake things up and find a workable solution.

Tuesday 24th

Today will feel unreal and you'll wonder if you dreamed it all. Conversations with a loved one can be intense. You may both drift off into fantasy land and speak two different languages. Misunderstandings need to be cleared up by evening or be left to fester and get worse.

Wednesday 25th

Mercury and Neptune face each other. This can mean that you hear gossip or expose someone for a liar. The Moon in your active, intimate sector is aggressive and needs to see some action. Unfortunately, with Mercury opposing Neptune, this can get nasty and you'll come off the worst.

Thursday 26th

You keep pushing for answers today. If you cannot compromise or make necessary changes, something will most certainly come to an end. This will not please you and you may fight against the injustice you perceive. Take some time to review what has happened before further action.

Friday 27th

The Moon shifts into your travel sector and the energy changes. You become stubborn and wilful. You make plans for a weekend of luxury. This is a knee-jerk reaction to recent events, and you will likely overspend, over-eat or take your sex drive too far. Try to be responsible today.

Saturday 28th

Today is likely to be purely hedonistic. You know what you want and will get it at all costs. The Moon meets Uranus while Venus connects also. Mars gets in on the act. This can be a sexy day or one driven by self-serving and sudden acts of passion.

Sunday 29th

Take a good look at your recent reactions to stress. The points of past and future karma have the Sun in a headlock. Clear your head and move forward in the best way possible, leaving the past behind. Your ruler spends his last day in your sign. Listening to your inner voice is important today.

Monday 30th

Your heart and head are quiet now. You may have moments where you regret recent actions. Let them be a lesson to you. Mercury enters your finance and value sector. He will talk your head off about getting back into balance in all parts of your life now.

Tuesday 31st

In the workplace, you may get irritated by unrealistic demands. It's not easy with Mars going through your sign. You're quick to anger and any connection to the Moon, like today, doesn't help. Keep things real and get all tasks done in your usual meticulous manner.

SEPTEMBER

. . . .

Wednesday 1st

The next few days will require you to exercise a little self-care.
Nurture yourself with what feeds your soul. Be with your
closest friends and listen to the wisdom of women around you.
Mercury tries to nudge you into being active, but you resist.
Lie low for the moment.

Thursday 2nd

Friendship groups can offer support if you're feeling down.
There may be pleasant surprises from unlikely people today.
Your emotions and ego are more comfortable however you do
feel guilty about wasting time. You don't have to be productive
all the time.

Friday 3rd

Your get up and go returns just in time for the weekend. You
find that you connect well to a partner and the energy is easy
between you. The only niggle comes from a desire to be cared
for without losing control of the situation. The Moon dips into
your hidden sector by evening, take it easy.

Saturday 4th

A connection to Mercury helps you to speak up and get a few
things off your chest. This may resolve an ongoing dispute
either from within you or with another. Unstable energy from
Saturn and Uranus act like the grit that forms a pearl. Use it to
find the precious gems in your psyche.

Sunday 5th

Venus is watching how you deal with irritation from your hidden sector. She gives you compassion and allows this healing not to disturb you too much. Conflict from an elder is possible. They may think you're neglecting your duties whilst you are doing your inner work. Ignore them.

Monday 6th

The Moon is in your sign and you feel more like yourself. Rising to a challenge may stimulate your mind and distract from your troubles. Watch that you don't get into power struggles coming from your creative sector. Use this energy to transform a project that has been on the back-burner.

Tuesday 7th

A New Moon in your sign gives you a wonderful opportunity to make goals and intentions purely about yourself and your personal growth. You may upset a few people by being more assertive than usual. When the Moon meets Mars in your sign your energy picks up and you're good to go.

Wednesday 8th

Aim for a day of balance. Check your finances, declutter and find order from chaos. This could be as simple as doing your laundry or getting a haircut. Doing responsible adult chores today will satisfy you greatly. A sense of calm is reached by evening. Well done.

Thursday 9th

Your heart and mind have a chat today. Listen carefully to see whether they are in agreement or not. There's no urgency to correct this now but make note of it for another time. Take another look at outstanding projects. Let them go if they're not pleasing you.

Friday 10th

The Moon and Venus meet up today just before Venus leaves your finances and values sector. Use this time to ensure that you have balanced your bank account and know what it is you want next. Keep it simple and take small steps to achieve the bigger life goal desired.

Saturday 11th

Conversations and short trips may be intense today. Your weekend could consist of intimate chats with siblings. Secrets may be revealed, and you learn something new which may shock you. This is a good time to share dreams and visions with a loved one. Try not to upset an elder.

Sunday 12th

Family time can be fun today as these are often lively times when you get together. Your energy can deal with children and older people in the same room. However, be careful not to go over the top with the entertainment or agree to do something you would rather not.

Monday 13th

You may be torn between family and a lover today. Have patience with a difficult person or ask them to be patient with you. You have the gift of the gab today as your ruler helps you mediate between people you love. Try to stay as objective as possible.

Tuesday 14th

The Sun sits opposite Neptune today. This has the effect of burning away any fog that Neptune has created. People in your intimate relationships may be seen in their true colours now. If someone is not as they once seemed, don't take your misjudgement of them personally.

Wednesday 15th

Mars leaves your sign to concentrate on building up the momentum of your earning power. This is also a good time to do a big DIY job such as demolition and restructuring part of your home. You may need to build a plan and talk it through with a partner today.

Thursday 16th

The Moon meets Pluto in your creative sector today and you can review projects, including love affairs. How much of an emotional attachment do you have? If you're being unrealistic or find that something is taking up space, you can now let it go with love and compassion.

Friday 17th

This is a difficult day. You may be pulled up and questioned about your duties and obligations. Women may come across as nasty and spiteful. Tempers can flare if you're not careful. Have you been neglecting your everyday chores recently? You may be judged on this today.

Saturday 18th

The Moon meets Jupiter and makes any mood you are in larger. The good news is that the Moon energy asks you to be altruistic and share the love. The bad news is that Jupiter in retrograde may make you rebellious at this time. Keep a low profile if you must.

Sunday 19th

Your intimate relationships are calling for your attention now. This may be the excuse you need to enjoy being with someone who understands your shadow side and yearning for a higher connection. A crisis of conscience can overtake your mind, but Venus helps you process your deep emotions.

Monday 20th

There is a Full Moon in your relationship sector tonight. This can be a dreamy time filled with your hopes and visions of the last six months. Neptune asks that you find your inner compass and re-orientate to your true north if you're not where you planned to be.

Tuesday 21st

Your inquiring mind needs to go deep today. There are discussions you need to have with someone very close to you. You must act considerately if you wish to get to know someone on a new level. It's possible that you come across as pushy or aggressive now.

Wednesday 22nd

Today is the Autumn Equinox. Day and night are equal lengths, so this is a good time to reflect. Look at how far you have come this year and where you would like to go next. Don't make any moves yet but get an action plan together.

Thursday 23rd

Your head may be spinning out of control today. It's tough trying to express yourself as you try too hard and put the other person on guard. Venus and Uranus are in opposition making your ideas about what is yours and what is shared quite unclear. There may be rows.

Friday 24th

If ever there is one of those days where you simply want to get away, this is it. You are feeling restricted by Saturn in your duties sector. The Moon connects with unstable Uranus making you volatile. Thankfully, this phase will pass soon. You simply have to ride it out.

Saturday 25th

Mercury goes retrograde tomorrow so use today to get everything in order. Back up all your devices and double-check all travel plans. This will happen in your finance sector. As Mercury is connected to commerce, take extra care and don't sign any contracts for this period.

Sunday 26th

Mercury retrograde begins. The Moon enters Mercury's sign and as it's your ruler, you may feel the effects more than most. However, the Moon makes helpful connections to the Sun and Mars also in your finance sector. Start this retrograde on a positive note and aim to review financial obligations.

Monday 27th

A tricky connection from the Moon to Neptune means that you may not be able to see through a problem. There is an answer, but it's evading you right now. Don't let it take up all your brain space today. Come back to it another time with fresh eyes.

Tuesday 28th

Tonight is the perfect time to allow yourself to be nurtured. Have some downtime with a close female friend or a mother. Let them look after you or treat each other to a wholesome meal. Listen to the advice of older women and let your intuition be your guide today.

Wednesday 29th

Mars is trying to nudge you out of your comfort zone today. Resist if you can but if you follow his call, use Uranus' energy to turn it to your advantage. You may come up with a new idea and want to run with it instantly. This may feed your soul.

Thursday 30th

Venus and Neptune connect in their watery signs to help you merge on a very deep level with a lover or a spiritual movement. The Moon adds more watery energy from your friendship sector. A midweek social evening or some time spent in meditation will satisfy your needs.

OCTOBER

. . . .

Friday 1st

The Moon drops into your hidden sector. You may feel emotionally drained as it opposes Saturn which can feel like a lead weight. However, nice connections to Mars and the Sun both in your money and values sector means that you can have a cheery night alone if needed.

Saturday 2nd

It's possible that you feel a little tearful today. Uranus is making you unstable as he dredges up more stuff from your psyche. A connection to your ruler, Mercury, helps you to process your private thoughts. Venus and Pluto help you transform outdated ways of thinking and feeling.

Sunday 3rd

This morning the Moon enters your own sign and gives you back personal strength. You can be methodical and rational about deep feelings. Assessing past and future karma will keep your mind occupied. Keep your notebook and checklists handy as you'll need them when your mind does overtime.

Monday 4th

Neptune attempts to draw you back into fantasy thinking. You may see yourself through the eyes of another, possibly a lover as Neptune is in your relationship sector. There may even be a pleasant surprise there when you realise just how much you are admired for your natural qualities.

Tuesday 5th

Transformations come easily today. The lord of change, Pluto, lets you see how a few tweaks to your current ways of thinking makes things better. This may solve a problem you've been struggling with. Venus communicates deep and intense knowledge of self-love to you. Secret yearnings rise up and are spoken aloud.

Wednesday 6th

A New Moon meets Mars. This is a time to make goals about finances and values as they will surely stick. Pluto turns direct today, adding conviction to these intentions. Out with the old and in with the new. The Moon then meets Mercury retrograde who files these intentions away.

Thursday 7th

Venus glides into your family sector. Watch how she brings harmony to this area now. The Moon enters the sign she has just left and your conversations will be strange. You're emotionally drawn to talking about life's mysteries and the taboo. Secrets may be shared between siblings.

Friday 8th

The Sun and Mars meet up today making a powerhouse of energy in your finance and values sector. You cannot miss the chance to use this energy and attract cash. You may have a great new money-making scheme ready to implement. This influence can also make you show off.

Saturday 9th

Tread carefully today, as the planetary energy is wild. You may have a ghost from the past come to visit you. Arguments are likely as Mercury bumps backwards into Mars. The Moon and Venus meet to smooth this over but instead, this connection makes you vulnerable to attack.

Sunday 10th

Saturn turns direct today and this will feel like a weight off your shoulders. Someone may have been relying too heavily on you over this period. If you have been overloaded with extra obligations you will see some fall away now. Perhaps a period of struggle has come to a natural end.

Monday 11th

A happy, outgoing Moon in your family sector brings you some joy today. You may be making plans for travel or a family adventure. Keep this idea burning as it may be a future activity which will open up the world to you and your kin.

Tuesday 12th

The Moon is now in your creative sector. Step by step you're achieving a milestone. Perhaps you haven't noticed this. Art, poetry, and love affairs all take time to perfect. Is this happening now? Genius thinking gives you a heads up in the right direction. How are you different from your peers?

Wednesday 13th

Patience must be exercised today as the Moon connects to Neptune. You may be in a rush to climb a mountain but you must remember to enjoy the view. Pluto shows you what you need to strip away and lighten your load. Make each step count.

Thursday 14th

The Moon meets newly direct Saturn today. This may feel like you're stepping into the headmaster's office with anticipation. Fear not, you're going to get some praise. Venus sends you optimism and courage. Uranus' rumblings are the butterflies you feel in your stomach. Fear is an illusion today.

Friday 15th

Sun and Moon both connect to Jupiter today. Ego and emotions can be larger than life. Try to remain calm and kind as others may push your buttons and try getting you to react. Rebelliousness doesn't suit you, it will make you look like a sulky child.

Saturday 16th

Have a quiet day with a lover or an important person. The Moon is free of connections to planets but does connect to the karmic points. You may be dreamy and idealistic today and this is harmless. Reminiscing about the past fills your Saturday nicely. You can be whimsical too.

Sunday 17th

Jupiter turns direct today. This also comes as a relief. Your health and duties sector has taken a bashing this year. Your inner voice has something to say to you today so make sure that you listen. Merging and connecting to a lover is getting easier now. Enjoy this time.

Monday 18th

Now Mercury turns direct. Your tricky ruler will retrace his steps in your finance and values sector once more. You should know by now which area you need to deal with differently. Perhaps a home makeover didn't work out quite as well as planned and needs to be re-done.

Tuesday 19th

The Moon in your intimacy sector is the first to contact Mercury today. They face off and you must try to sift through emotional and logical processes. Feeling and thinking are difficult to reconcile. Mars and Jupiter both want you to err on the side of reason.

Wednesday 20th

You may be unsure how to proceed with any plans you've been harbouring for a while now. Forget those and look at what you have achieved this year. A Full Moon in your intimacy sector shows you if shared finances or deep relating has come to anything. Celebrate your gains.

Thursday 21st

In your travel sector, the Moon meets Uranus. It's very likely that you make an impulse purchase which is expensive or luxurious. This can include suddenly taking off for an adventure. Saturn is watching with a stern brow. You will regret this at a later date.

Friday 22nd

You are very tempted to follow an impossible dream today. Be sensible, this could be disastrous. Mars and Pluto are at odds and you don't want the planets of war and permanent endings to influence any rash decision you make now. Wait until the energy gives you a green light.

Saturday 23rd

The Sun enters your communications sector now. You will find that your everyday conversations become more interesting and light up your brain cells with many ideas. You will explore the darker side of life now that the light shines on it. This makes you feel safer as you enter unknown waters.

Sunday 24th

The Moon in your career sector opposes Venus today. You may see a conflict between men and women, fathers and mothers, or workers and homemakers. When the two feminine planets face off, there's a chance that gossip and jealousy are afoot. Be mindful that this doesn't involve you.

Monday 25th

Your mind will be so busy today that you welcome a quiet retreat by evening. A late-night conversation with a close friend or a chat on social media helps you to wind down. Before you sleep you'll feel more positive but still mentally active.

Tuesday 26th

Venus and Neptune are at odds today. Families and lovers both demand your time. The best thing you can do is avoid both and enjoy time to yourself or with your online friends. You must protect your energy and stay in your comfort zone or risk being angered and defensive.

Wednesday 27th

Another difficult day. You may see control issues or power struggles coming from your love affairs. Speak up clearly and show them the boundaries. Your heart needs you to lie low with familiar things around you whilst your head is busy trying to keep the peace with people close to you.

Thursday 28th

The energy picks up and you are allowed some peace. The Moon enters your private sector where for once you enjoy the silence. You have no need to roar and be heard. Venus and Jupiter combine to quieten your family and other obligations or at least make them joyful.

Friday 29th

Whilst in your private sector, the Moon reflects light on your dark areas. You aren't too happy about dealing with this today. Gentle whisperings from your ruler Mercury enable you to sift through them and decide which are necessary and which to deal with at another time.

Saturday 30th

Mars enters your communications sector. You will be driven and forceful with him here. There will be no stone unturned and no secret left preserved. In his own sign, he is ruthless. You can do all your detective work now and get to the bottom of the deepest mystery.

Sunday 31st

The Moon is in your sign and you're a force to be reckoned with today. The selfless servant of everyone is taking a stand. Watch whose noses you put out of joint now as this will tell you a lot about who takes you for granted. Say what you mean now.

NOVEMBER

. . . .

Monday 1st

Your mind is on fire today. Mercury and Jupiter connect to help you get things in order on a grand scale. Neptune beckons you to switch off but you ignore the call and multi-task like a professional. Changes or endings can be made now with very little regret.

Tuesday 2nd

Forward motion may be hindered by something unforeseen today. You may have to rethink a strategy or find balance in another way. Saturn watches how you handle this and gives you the benefit of wisdom to deal with this in a responsible, adult way. It will all turn out well.

Wednesday 3rd

Pluto is still influencing your mood and productivity today. You may feel emotionally attached to something you need to let go. This could be money, investments or property. The Moon and Mercury have a chat and you'll need to dissociate feelings from logic and reason. Jupiter makes your emotions larger.

Thursday 4th

A New Moon in your communications sector asks you to do the detective work necessary. This is a tricky day with a lot of planetary energies which can make you unstable. Venus is about to leave your family sector. You must get to the root of any problems now.

Friday 5th

The Sun sits opposite Uranus today. This acts like a light bulb moment where you get clarity and maybe a genius solution to a difficult situation. Mercury flies into your communications sector where he will be your best ally. Expect a lot of deep conversations and short trips now.

Saturday 6th

Enjoy this weekend with family. Elders need your love and attention and you will be happy to give it. A love affair may be starting for you. Mercury talks to Venus the planet of love who is in your creative sector now. Expressions of love come easily.

Sunday 7th

You may feel that you have a lot of duties now but remember that you have also shed some. Family comes first today, and you approach all that you need to do with optimism and joy. Your altruistic nature comes out, making you happy to serve those who need you.

Monday 8th

The Moon is making amazing connections today. She sits in your creative sector generating energy, conversations, love and surprise moments. This is a lucky day for you. Your divine essence shines through and you attract all the right people. Fill your heart and let it overflow to others.

Tuesday 9th

You may struggle with issues of control as the Moon meets Pluto. However, this could highlight a need to check in with your emotions. You have let a lot go recently, perhaps you are just pausing to think about how that makes you feel. Neptune lets you listen to your inner voice.

Wednesday 10th

Mercury and Mars meet up and their effect has you running around at full speed. Chores, messages and visits are all achieved easily with these two behind you. You may not like it very much and will vocalise this to whoever listens. Be productive and don't sulk.

Thursday 11th

The Moon meets Jupiter today. You could be blowing your own trumpet and inflating yourself with pride. Showing off about how much you can do with efficiency isn't a good idea. You are noticed and appreciated for what you do, there's no need to point it out.

Friday 12th

Your lover or special person will need your attention over the weekend. This is an excellent time to switch off and enjoy some downtime. You may feel at a crossroads, but this is a passing phase and will be over soon. Venus wants you to merge with your lover or spirit.

Saturday 13th

You may contemplate the acts of surrender and sacrifice and what they mean to you in a partnership Your sexual energy and art of conversation are both on a roll. You can win someone over now. Be careful not to talk about risky subjects too soon.

Sunday 14th

After a time of connection, you desire to make plans and strategies to merge deeper. You may need to slow down. Be mindful of personal boundaries and don't push another person out of their comfort zone. Tread carefully and keep your plans on the back-burner for a later date.

Monday 15th

It's likely that you see conflict arise between men and women today. Egos and emotions are not in sync with traditional gender roles, causing disturbances or bullying between the sexes. This is in your more personal areas of life and not your wider world. Remember to be responsible and respectful.

Tuesday 16th

The battles continue to occur in your intimate and love sectors. Jupiter tries to help by connecting to the Moon and asking you to see out the truth of a matter. Jupiter loves justice and sits in your health and duties sector. A wise elder may give impartial advice today.

Wednesday 17th

With Mars and Uranus in opposition, anything could happen. Your sectors of communication and travel will be explosive today as these two volatile planets face off. This could be an all-out war or highly productive time. Either way, protect yourself from the fall-out and try not to get exhausted.

Thursday 18th

The Moon is now involved in this war. You will be emotionally charged and may need to reluctantly take a side. You ask for help from Neptune, beg him to take you away from it all. You may wish to shut the door and wrap yourself up in a blanket.

Friday 19th

A Full Moon in your travel sector appears to be the culmination of the recent difficult energy. You can make a last-ditch attempt to detach yourself from other people's dramas. Treat yourself with tasty exotic food and remind yourself of your desire to travel. Set your mind onto a different path.

Saturday 20th

Have a day with your thoughts. The Moon in your career sector gives you space and time to process a lot of information today. You may be researching for work or pleasure. Mercury whispers something to Jupiter in your duties sector, he says he's not available to others today.

Sunday 21st

Your mind is still busy. You may be following many different threads of enquiry. Don't take on too many as you will become overloaded and ultimately indecisive. You attend only to the most important of duties today. Let them be the ones that make you smile.

Monday 22nd

The Sun moves into your vibrant family sector today. Expect the seasonal festivities to begin now. You're protective of your energy and only allow those who you are very close to break down your barriers. Social activities may drain you as you are somewhat vulnerable to attack.

Tuesday 23rd

You're being called out of hiding by a potential lover. You desire to respond but need to hide out a little longer. This stirs your sexual energy and will keep you at just the right temperature until the time is right. Make do with fantasies and dreams for now.

Wednesday 24th

Mercury is at the final degree of your communications sector. If you need to make contact, then it's crucial that you do so now. You must step out of your cave and be bold. This evening the Moon shifts into your private sector which is ruled by courageous Leo.

Thursday 25th

Don't back out of any plans which take you beyond your comfort zone, they will do you good. Venus and Mars are close to making a great connection between your communications and creative sector. This energy is too good to miss. Find your best clothes and get ready.

Friday 26th

The Moon opposes Jupiter while in your hidden sector. You may have a moment of crisis and believe that you're not worthy or not good enough. This is fear talking, don't listen. You're being given the opportunity to shine in all your glory, take it.

Saturday 27th

The Moon dips into your sign and your confidence rises. However, your communications are lacking the fire to back this up. Use your Virgo powers and make a checklist. Prepare a speech with crib notes if necessary. Check every detail of any plan put forward to you now.

Sunday 28th

The butterflies in your stomach are making you twitchy. Fantasy driven Neptune calls you from your relationship sector, but you're refusing to go there. You feel much safer in your own territory. Stick with it, this nervous energy will dissipate soon and you will be grounded once more.

Monday 29th

You feel much more balanced today and the voices in your head are calmed. This is due to Mercury, your chatty ruler, being in the heat of the Sun. This is a good time to listen to the one, true, guiding voice and ignore your inner critic. Sexy Mars is ready for love.

Tuesday 30th

Today you may be more moody than usual. The Moon makes an unhelpful connection to Venus and you may be overemotional. This will pass quickly. Many other planetary connections suggest that the energy is right for you to enjoy some fun, laughter and love. You deserve this.

DECEMBER

. . . .

Wednesday 1st

Neptune turns direct today. This is great news if you've been too idealistic and unrealistic in your partnerships. You will now have clarity and see falsity dissolve before your eyes. You may have been wearing rose-tinted glasses or projecting your own issues onto another. This will be exposed.

Thursday 2nd

A deeply communicative Moon makes you do all the right research and investigations about highly sensitive subjects. There is much you want to know and learn. Be careful that you don't probe too deeply as you wander into sensitive areas you're not ready for.

Friday 3rd

Mars and the Moon meet up today. Sex drive is high and a romantic evening is likely. However, this can also lead to passive-aggression. The Moon squares off with Jupiter so be mindful that you don't push boundaries too far. By evening you are more family orientated but still outgoing and cheerful.

Saturday 4th

A New Moon in your family sector is a great chance to check in with your loved ones and make sure everyone is OK. There may be members who need their spirits lifted. You wear your heart on your sleeve today and whatever comes out of your mouth is truly heartfelt.

Sunday 5th

Your mood is buoyant, and you're ready for anything that is thrown at you. This afternoon, you slow down and decide that any progression in your creative sector, including love affairs, needs to be taken one step at a time. This is not a bad thing.

Monday 6th

You're determined and steadfast today. Taking a good look at all your responsibilities is time well spent. You can be highly organised as the Moon makes helpful connections to planets which are usually distracting or volatile. Mars and Pluto connect to help you tear down old values.

Tuesday 7th

The Moon now connects to both Pluto and Mars. They are clearing the way for new ways of thinking, creating and relating to come in. The Moon shifts into your health and duties sector. Check in with your body now and do something for yourself. Assess your diet and exercise regimes.

Wednesday 8th

Today may be tricky as you come up against conflict from an elder or boss. This energy could also mean that you're being too hard on yourself, you are your own boss after all. You may not feel so good. Tears and tantrums may not be far away.

Thursday 9th

Have you possibly burnt out? The Moon meets Jupiter but also squares off with Mars. Your energy may be depleted. Take some time to pause and be good to yourself. A family member may offer advice. Listen to what they have to say, it will be valuable.

Friday 10th

The Moon floats into your relationship sector giving you a chance to switch off and relax with a loved one. Simple energy allows you to treat both of you to a tasty dinner or a great film. You're restless but in a nice way. This means that something has touched you.

Saturday 11th

Venus and Pluto meet in your creative sector. You will likely see control issues and power struggles today. Other Moon connections suggest that you take an objective view and do nothing. Detach yourself from the drama and let others deal with it. Don't speak your mind today.

Sunday 12th

Venus and Pluto are still having trouble agreeing today. Are you too attached to something which needs to change or be ended? What is it you're trying to hang on to? Take a peek into your relationship sector as the Sun is making a tough connection to Neptune's illusions.

Monday 13th

Mercury enters your creative sector with many ideas and words of love. Mars also changes signs. He marches into your family sector. He will pull up the stragglers and get everyone ready for an adventure. The Moon makes you emotionally deep and intense but with lots of ideas for intimate evenings.

Tuesday 14th

Your travel sector is highlighted and you feel that familiar pull towards unknown territory. Have you had a holiday this year? Perhaps you're regretting not getting away often enough. You fill your mind with far-reaching plans to visit lands that can tantalise your senses.

Wednesday 15th

You're restless today. Elders or people in authority may be giving you some pressure. When the Moon meets Uranus that pressure is likely to blow up in your face. Toe the line and concentrate on your work. Do what it takes to get through the day without conflict.

Thursday 16th

Today you find a way to make those difficult changes or let attachments go. Neptune helps you to dissolve any illusions you've been harbouring whilst Venus sends you love and peace to do so. Take it slowly and process your feelings. You will soon see the benefits of this.

Friday 17th

Your mind is extra busy. Maybe you're bringing work home with you for the weekend. This will cause friction with your family time and you will need to find a happy balance. Stay disciplined and alert today and over the weekend. Keep emotions away from rational decisions now.

Saturday 18th

Neptune is asking you to switch off, but you cannot spare the time. If you're to enjoy the festivities then you must do the extra work now. This isn't easy at this time of year. You may have to decline a party invitation and keep your mind on your tasks.

Sunday 19th

Venus turns retrograde today. This will be a period where love affairs are disrupted, and you may see a face from the past return. A Full Moon in your career sector highlights all that you have been working towards this year. The extra work has paid off.

Monday 20th

The Moon in your social sector brings some light relief. It opposes Mercury who asks you to mind your words and not risk upsetting friends. Alcohol can loosen tongues and cause problems. As Uranus is involved here too, let his restlessness bring a good time and not conflict.

Tuesday 21st

The Winter Solstice occurs today. This is a time to pause and reflect on the year gone by. Try to find a pivot and maintain balance if just for now. The days will shorten and the darker months are upon you. How will you fill up the long, dark nights?

Wednesday 22nd

The Moon is in your hidden sector. You may need to have some time alone and recharge ready for the upcoming celebrations. Family members may try to call you out of hiding but you must decline. Do only what is necessary and keep your energy for the next few days.

Thursday 23rd

Jupiter has come back to the final degree of your health and duties sector. This planet of joy and expansion asks that you have gone as far as you can go in this area. How is your health? Are you mentally well or exhausted? Make a note to review this.

Friday 24th

The Moon drops into your sign this morning. You will find that you're required for your organising skills. This may cause you some grief as you feel you're being taken for granted. Make sure that you have the energy to comply or you will not enjoy the celebrations.

Saturday 25th

Control issues and power struggles are most evident today. Venus has met Pluto again in your creative sector. You may have to surrender the control to someone just to keep the peace. Don't sacrifice yourself, just go with the flow and do what is asked of you.

Sunday 26th

You're emotionally involved with the power struggles in your creative sector but you're handling them well. The Moon in your sign makes good connections. It's possible that you're taking charge and being as objective as possible. Your keen eye for detail may save the day.

Monday 27th

The Moon is in your finances and value sector. You know your worth and are able to get this across to others today. You can be strict and assertive without upsetting anyone. You may be called on for your wisdom in making balanced decisions about money. Be responsible and don't overspend.

Tuesday 28th

You will need to be firm but fair with someone today. The Moon makes hard connections to the planets in your creative sector. This is another day where you must stand up for your right to be who you are without filters. Venus and Pluto make it challenging.

Wednesday 29th

The Moon in your communications sector gives you trouble speaking to authority figures today. There is a possibility of a tantrum or an upsetting episode where you don't get your own way. Look to your own behaviour and own it. Lucky Jupiter enters your relationship sector for the next year.

Thursday 30th

You have the gift of the gab and can talk anyone around to your way of thinking today. Mercury meets Pluto and as your ruler, he assists you in being persuasive. You can do this with love and compassion and avoid unnecessary conflict. Well done.

Friday 31st

The end of the year is here. The Moon sits with the point of past karma and you look back at how much you've lost and achieved this year. The Moon also meets Mars and gives you the emotional energy to party all night and see the new year in.

Virgo

PEOPLE WHO
SHARE YOUR SIGN

. . . .

The valuable influence of warm and hard-working Virgoans can be felt in the smallest and largest of ways, from helping just one friend to serving the masses. From perfectionist performers such as Beyoncé to Nobel Peace Prize winners such as Mother Teresa, Virgoans have the capacity to guide and inspire. Discover the public figures who share your exact birthday and see if you can spot the similarities.

24th August

Rupert Grint (1988), Chad Michael Murray (1981), John Green (1977), Alex O'Loughlin (1976), Dave Chappelle (1973), Ava DuVernay (1972), Marlee Matlin (1965), Stephen Fry (1957), Vince McMahon (1945)

25th August

Blake Lively (1987), Rachel Bilson (1981), Alexander Skarsgård (1976), Ben Falcone (1973), Claudia Schiffer (1970), Billy Ray Cyrus (1961), Tim Burton (1958), Gene Simmons (1949), Sean Connery (1930), Faustina Kowalska (1905)

26th August

Keke Palmer (1993), Dylan O'Brien (1991), James Harden (1989), Evan Ross (1988), Macaulay Culkin (1980), Chris Pine (1980), Amanda Schull (1978), Melissa McCarthy (1970), Mother Teresa (1910)

27th August

Alexa Vega (1988), Patrick J. Adams (1981), Aaron Paul (1979), Suranne Jones (1978), Sarah Chalke (1976), Mark Webber (1976), Tom Ford (1961), Peter Stormare (1953), Paul Reubens (1952), Barbara Bach (1947), Lyndon B. Johnson, U.S. President (1908)

28th August

Armie Hammer (1986), Florence Welch (1986), LeAnn Rimes (1982), Jack Black (1969), Sheryl Sandberg (1969), Shania Twain (1965), David Fincher (1962), Jennifer Coolidge (1961)

29th August

Liam Payne (1993), Lea Michele (1986), Carla Gugino (1971), Lenny Henry (1958), Temple Grandin (1947), James Hunt (1947), Iris Apfel (1921), Ingrid Bergman (1915)

30th August

Trevor Jackson (1996), Bebe Rexha (1989), Johanna Braddy (1987), Cameron Diaz (1972), Michael Chiklis (1963), Warren Buffett (1930), Ernest Rutherford (1871)

31st August

Sara Ramirez (1975), Chris Tucker (1971), Queen Rania of Jordan (1970), Tsai Ing-wen, President of the Republic of China (1956), Marcia Clark (1953), Richard Gere (1949), Van Morrison (1945), Georg Jensen (1866)

1st September

Zendaya (1996), Daniel Sturridge (1989), Chanel West Coast (1988), Boyd Holbrook (1981), Gloria Estefan (1957), Dr Phil McGraw (1950), Barry Gibb (1946), Lily Tomlin (1939)

2nd September

Alexandre Pato (1989), Zedd (1989), Salma Hayek (1966), Lennox Lewis (1965), Keanu Reeves (1964), Eugenio Derbez (1961), Mark Harmon (1951), Robert Shapiro (1942)

3rd September

Kaia Gerber (2001), Dominic Thiem (1993), Shaun White (1986), Garrett Hedlund (1984), Fearne Cotton (1981), Redfoo (1975), Charlie Sheen (1965), Malcolm Gladwell (1963), Jaggi Vasudev (1957)

4th September

Yannick Carrasco (1993), James Bay (1990), Beyoncé (1981), Max Greenfield (1979), Wes Bentley (1978), Mark Ronson (1975), Damon Wayans (1960), Dr Drew Pinsky (1958)

5th September

Giovanni Pernice (1990), Kat Graham (1989), Annabelle Wallis (1984), Carice van Houten (1976), Rose McGowan (1973), Michael Keaton (1951), Freddie Mercury (1946), Raquel Welch (1940), Jesse James (1847)

6th September

Lauren Lapkus (1985), Pippa Middleton (1983), Kerry Katona (1980), Naomie Harris (1976), Idris Elba (1972), Anika Noni Rose (1972), Macy Gray (1967), Swoosie Kurtz (1944), Roger Waters (1943), Jane Addams (1860)

7th September

Evan Rachel Wood (1987), Oliver Hudson (1976), Shannon Elizabeth (1973), Leslie Jones (1967), Toby Jones (1966), Eazy-E (1964), Gloria Gaynor (1949), Buddy Holly (1936)

8th September

Cameron Dallas (1994), Joe Sugg (1991), Avicii (1989), Wiz Khalifa (1987), P!nk (1979), David Arquette (1971), Martin Freeman (1971), Bernie Sanders (1941), Antonín Dvořák (1841)

9th September

Luka Modrić (1985), Zoe Kazan (1983), Michelle Williams (1980), Michael Bublé (1975), Adam Sandler (1966), Hugh Grant (1960), Colonel Sanders (1890), Leo Tolstoy (1828)

10th September

Ryan Phillippe (1974), Guy Ritchie (1968), Jack Ma (1964), Colin Firth (1960), Joe Perry (1950), Bill O'Reilly (1949), Cynthia Lennon (1939), Mary Oliver (1935), Karl Lagerfeld (1933)

11th September

Kygo (1991), Tyler Hoechlin (1987), Ludacris (1977), Taraji P. Henson (1970), Harry Connick Jr. (1967), Moby (1965), Scott Patterson (1958)

12th September

Connor Franta (1992), Alfie Allen (1986), Emmy Rossum (1986), Jennifer Hudson (1981), Ben McKenzie (1979), Paul Walker (1973), Hans Zimmer (1957), Barry White (1944), Jesse Owens (1913)

13th September

Niall Horan (1993), Ben Savage (1980), Fabio Cannavaro (1973), Stella McCartney (1971), Tyler Perry (1969), Dave Mustaine (1961), Jacqueline Bisset (1944), Roald Dahl (1916)

14th September

Jessica Brown Findlay (1989), Amy Winehouse (1983), Ben Cohen (1978), Andrew Lincoln (1973), Nas (1973), Sam Neill (1947), Margaret Sanger (1879)

15th September

Jenna Marbles (1986), Prince Harry, Duke of Sussex (1984), Tom Hardy (1977), Jimmy Carr (1972), Queen Letizia of Spain (1972), Tommy Lee Jones (1946), Agatha Christie (1890), William Howard Taft, U.S. President (1857)

16th September

Nick Jonas (1992), Alexis Bledel (1981), Amy Poehler (1971), Marc Anthony (1968), Molly Shannon (1964), Mickey Rourke (1952), Peter Falk (1927), B.B. King (1925), Lauren Bacall (1924)

17th September

Melissa Hemsley (1985), Flo Rida (1979), Anastasia (1968), Cheryl Strayed (1968), Kyle Chandler (1965), Narendra Modi, Indian Prime Minister (1950), John Ritter (1948), Jim Rohn (1930), Hank Williams (1923), Billy the Kid (1859)

18th September

Patrick Schwarzenegger (1993), Ronaldo (1976), Jason Sudeikis (1975), Xzibit (1974), James Marsden (1973), Jada Pinkett Smith (1971), Aisha Tyler (1970), James Gandolfini (1961), John McAfee (1945)

19th September

Danielle Panabaker (1987), Lauren Goodger (1986), Skepta (1982), Jimmy Fallon (1974), Sanaa Lathan (1971), Lita Ford (1958), Twiggy (1949), Jeremy Irons (1948), Adam West (1928)

20th September

Phillip Phillips (1990), Jon Bernthal (1976), Victor Ponta, Romanian Prime Minister (1972), Michelle Visage (1968), Kristen Johnston (1967), George R. R. Martin (1948), Sophia Loren (1934), Anne Meara (1929), Upton Sinclair (1878)

21st September

Jason Derulo (1989), Maggie Grace (1983), Nicole Richie (1981), Liam Gallagher (1972), Alfonso Ribeiro (1971), Luke Wilson (1971), Faith Hill (1967), Abby Lee Miller (1966), Shinzō Abe, Japanese Prime Minister (1954), Bill Murray (1950), Stephen King (1947), Leonard Cohen (1934)

22nd September

Daniela Ospina (1992), Tom Felton (1987), Thiago Silva (1984), Billie Piper (1982), Sue Perkins (1969), Andrea Bocelli (1958), Joan Jett (1958), Nick Cave (1957), Rosamunde Pilcher (1924)

23rd September

Anthony Mackie (1978), Karl Pilkington (1972), Jason Alexander (1959), Bruce Springsteen (1949), Julio Iglesias (1943), Romy Schneider (1938), Ray Charles (1930), Mickey Rooney (1920)